ENDORSEMENTS FOR

USED TO GO TO CHURCH

"I cannot say how profoundly comforting and rewarding it is to read someone who is not theorizing about the problem of suffering. An author who 'sits with you' in the traumas and tragedies of life—and does not 'leave the room' with religious platitudes. Real, raw, gritty—and life-giving. If you have experienced or been near intense loss, I recommend this book for you."

— **Dr. Bruce McNicol**, Co-author, *The Cure* and *The Ascent of a Leader*, Co-founder, Trueface

"If you think you need to be in church every Sunday to restore your faith in God, think again. Nick's lifelong devotion to God combined with his work as a first responder chaplain make his spiritual observations compelling and challenging. He gives us an understanding of how God works in times of tragedy, helping us to better process and heal following such horrific events."

— **William Enquist**, Global President, Medical Device Company

"*Used to Go to Church* was a great read and seeks to answer a lot of the questions surrounding why we sometimes leave the church. Exploring answers to why over time, we become more skeptical about what we learned in the Church. I found it a great read that allowed me to think introspectively about my own path of starting off with faith, leaving the church and ultimately coming back to my faith even stronger than before. *Used to Go to Church* provides real and practical examples of why God and his message are important in our daily lives."

— **Allan Shields**, Chief of Police

"This book is real, gritty and the author understands grief with no canned Sunday School answers. A must read for anyone who has ever experienced a crushing life trauma, heartache or disappointment that shakes you to your core. Nick will challenge you, because in doing so, the Lord will use his words to change you.

I learned something about myself and about my Savior in reading *Used to Go to Church*. The Lord is calling us back to Him.

I see now, He was with me in moments of personal crisis and isolation. He was with me in my tears, depression and it was his unseen hand that lovingly and patiently led me out of the spiritual darkness. When I felt most alone, it was his unseen presence that kept me alive and gave me hope. His mercies and faithfulness are new every day."

– **Steve Wisniewski**, former 13-year All-Pro NFL
Player, LA / Oakland Raiders 1989-2001

"Reading through *Used to Go to Church* is one of the most excruciating—and rewarding—experiences of my life. Nick's ability to capture a scene, an emotion—a swirl of conflicting emotions, and all the questions, all the agony that accompanies that kinds of crises that he describes with such excruciating immediacy, intimacy and accuracy—is a gift that makes me want to run away and hide. And yet, at the same time, wakes me up and sends me in the direction of people in pain. It's almost too much, because it's too real. But it is the world that firefighters, police officers and paramedics, as well as many schoolteachers, counselors, coaches and pastors know well. And so do you, if your eyes and ears and heart are open.

This isn't theory, this is reality. This isn't stained glass religion, this is faith in action—faith that goes down, gets bloody, discovers humanity at such a deep level, and encounters the God who shows up when we need what only God can provide: grace (the grace to be present without offering easy answers), strength (the strength to be vulnerable) and hope (that is willing to wait for the surprise of kindness that heals).

Nick is a wizened, experienced chaplain, a man's man, who remains open and honest, in a childlike way, and full of wonder at the intersection of suffering and love, of tragedy and miracle. He does not flinch in the telling nor rush to define or summarize all that he witnesses. But it seems he never fails to discover the sacred in the midst of the sadness, the fears and the temptation to despair. This is what he does, what he shares in this book, what he believes, almost defiantly, why he is a follower of Jesus, and what he calls people of faith to recognize and faithfully, compassionately practice. Don't miss this adventure—the invitation to read about it, learn to care about it, and eventually live into this beautiful, practical spirituality."

– **Doug Stevens**, Author of *Christ Incognito*

"I have known Nick my entire life. We went to kindergarten through high school together and remain close as brothers to this day. Upon reading his book, *Used to Go to Church*, I realized that I somehow missed the complete depth of my good friend. He has been called by God to perform the most difficult task anyone can be asked to do and has accepted this charge. His experiences are uniquely personal and truly inspirational. The spiritual insight gained from reading this book will challenge you and stay with you forever!"

— **Bill Springman**, MLB Player Development Coach

"This book is an easy engaging read that accurately shares the journey of an experienced Fire and Law enforcement Chaplain. Throughout his journey there is a tremendous amount of experience shared that is honest, authentic, and transparent. The real stories contained in this book share years of highs and lows and many lessons learned. The stories contained in this book describe many real emotional tragedies and the process the Chaplain used to professionally and compassionately work through them. Each chapter will encourage the reader provoking deep and personal spiritual thoughts. The book could potentially change one's perspective on their personal trials and tribulations, it did for me."

— **Brian Helmick**, Fire Chief

"Much of Nick's life work has been about building a bridge between how people experience 'the God of the church' as being irrelevant and the God they long to believe in when unimaginable tragedy and hardship enters their lives. It is a bridge built in the crucible of hundreds of unspeakable tragedies and grace-filled moments Nick has experienced in his years as first responder chaplain, as together with officers and firefighters, they meet with people in the moment of their worst nightmares.

With astonishing vulnerability, Nick shares with us his own faith journey as he wrestles with God around his own questions of 'why?', is present to people in their loss, cares for first responders in their own trauma, and navigates the realities of PTSD in his own life. It is not a book offering answers to hard questions; it is about believing in a God who also knows suffering and is not afraid to accompany us in ours.

This book will open your eyes to a reality lived around us each day: the trauma of personal and community tragedy *and* God's presence, grace and love, often made available to us through people like Nick. It has definitely opened my eyes and my heart."

— **Patti Pierce**, Founder of WellSpring: A Resource
for Christian Spiritual Formation

First Edition

Cover design and layout by Rafael Polendo (polendo.net). Cover image by storyblocks.com.

To protect the privacy of individuals, some names, locations, and identifying details may have been changed.

ISBN 978-1-938480-62-1

This volume is printed on acid free paper and meets ANSI Z39.48 standards.

Printed in the United States of America

 QUOIR

Published by Quoir
Orange, California

www.quoir.com

USED TO GO TO CHURCH

RETHINKING GOD ON THE FRONTLINE OF LIFE'S TRAGEDIES

NICK VLEISIDES
FIRST RESPONDER CHAPLAIN

TABLE OF CONTENTS

ACKNOWLEDGMENTS

After working alongside first responders—firefighters, officers, deputies, nurses, doctors—for many years I must give them a shout out and thank them for being an inspiration to me in ways that have helped me stay the course as a first responder chaplain without going nuts! They are amazing people who occasionally (which is too often) see things that no human being was ever intended to witness. You can not do this kind of work without it taking a bite out of your soul. I am so proud to work alongside these extraordinary human beings!

Thank you to all those of you who shared a most a sacred, precious time with me as a chaplain on scenes where a loved one of yours unexpectedly died. You have taught me much about what counts in life and revealed to me how love expresses itself in all kinds of relationships. I especially wish to dedicate this book to the many parents of young men and women, yes, even of boys and girls who took their own lives. My heart goes out to you and there is a part of me which is broken after experiencing first hand your unspeakable grief. But my life is much more real because of meeting you. May God give you peace.

My wife, Heidi, and my three adult children, Trent, Noelle and Trevor have endured watching a husband and father change over the years. Like most first responders I too have seen my heart of emotions become guarded and have experienced a sort of withdrawal from important relationships at times. It is hard to explain, but ask any family member of a cop, firefighter or ER nurse and they will tell you how they see their loved one as "not the same guy (or gal) they first married." Without my family to keep me honest and real, I would be lost. Thank you. I love you all so much!

Finally, I wish to thank author and friend Jim Palmer who I met after reading his book, *Divine Nobodies*. When I told him I was writing a book he asked to see the manuscript and immediately saw great potential in the impact it could have. He was gracious to offer feedback and input on the manuscript, and his encouragement was an invaluable part of the process of completing this book. Jim is a fellow soul, and we share a mutual desire and resolve to be instruments of love, hope, peace, compassion, and courage in the world.

FOREWORD

Fyodor Dostoyevsky wrote, "Suffering is a chance you take by the fact of being alive." People sometimes question the existence or character of God because of suffering in the world and the tragedies that inevitably befall our lives. However, we should at least acknowledge that God informed us that the human journey would be volatile, including such trials and tribulations as loss, disease, death, and heartbreaking experiences that make us weep. Lest we think that God has unfairly singled us out with hardship, few human beings will ever experience the psychological and physical suffering Jesus endured.

If there is anyone with reason to walk away from God on account of suffering, it would be Nick Vleisides. Frequently Nick is thrust into a world of heartbreak, tragedy, and some of the most gruesome scenes of death. For nearly 25 years Nick has been called to grim scenes, including a 13-year-old suicide, pool drowning of a toddler, domestic violence, homicide, gruesome vehicle accidents, deadly plane crash, suicides too many to count, and numerous teenage overdoses.

Nick is a first responder chaplain, which means he is called into horrific scenarios of death and loss, for the purpose of providing psychological, emotional and spiritual support to those affected by these tragedies. It was the 15-year-old boy's dad who found him hanging from a rope in his room. The toddler's mother pulled her little girl out of the backyard pool, but it was too late. Those who fled for their lives from the Paradise Fire in Northern California. There were people to notify that their loved ones had perished in a fire, and parents whose children would not be returning home from school. It was Nick's job to tell them, comfort them, be a human being of compassion and empathy and guide them through the initial steps of trauma recovery and processing their grief. On a regular basis, he sees the unbearable grief of others in those first few minutes of reckoning.

The work of a first responder chaplain also involves supporting other first responders such as paramedics, EMTs, police officers, firefighters, and rescuers, who are often traumatized by their direct involvement in gruesome scenes of death and loss of life. Nick was instrumental in starting the peer support teams for his fire and police departments. For every death on the scene of a fire there is a firefighter who feels some responsibility. For every unsuccessful attempt to revive a victim, there is a paramedic who feels a sense of failure. Police officers can never unsee the grim scene of a child run over by a car. Nick's role as a first responder chaplain is to be a source of understanding and support for these brave men and women.

The word "chaplain" in Nick's job title evokes the subject of God, and immerses him in the hurt, anger, betrayal and disillusionment people often feel toward God in the face of catastrophic loss. "How could God take my little girl?" "Why would God let my son die like this?" "Where is God?" These are a few of the desperate questions often asked of Nick in the moments of a person's greatest heartache and sorrow.

Despite Nick's theological background and years as a pastor before his career as a first responder chaplain, he discovered that questions about the meaning of tragedy and suffering, and where to find God in it, are not worked out with seminary answers or well-intended statements from church people like, "Your son is in a better place now", "God wanted her home" or "God will never give you more than you can handle".

Outside of Christian subculture in his work as a first responder chaplain, Nick found a discomforting disconnect between the church world of pop worship songs like "God is good all the time" and the realities of tragedy and suffering like school shootings and teen suicide. A recurrent response he received from those left behind at these scenes of overwhelming loss when he introduced himself as a chaplain was, "I used to go to church." Nick wondered if the pat answers and bumper-sticker theology of Churchianity contributed to this, as well as the failure of the church to be real about the struggles and hardships of the human journey, and wrestling with God's place in them.

If you are looking for easy and feel-good answers or bulletproof theological explanations to resolve the question of God and suffering on paper, this is not the book for you. And if you are expecting to be comforted by hearing what you have always been told in Church about such things, you may be displeased and perhaps even offended. But if you are interested in reading a story about one human being's journey to make sense of life and God on the frontlines of life's greatest tragedies, you will not be disappointed.

Nick's honesty and humanity in telling his story is moving. The world of first responders he shows is striking. The experiences he recounts are gripping.

The life and spiritual insights he shares are profound. Throughout the book you will be given perspectives that you have likely never contemplated and will be invited to consider God in ways that perhaps you never have. Whether you are religious or non-religious, Christian or agnostic, church-goer or church-leaver, the person who is starting with page one of *Used to Go to Church* will not be the same person who finishes the last sentence.

— **Jim Palmer,** Author of *Notes from (Over) the Edge*, and *Inner Anarchy*

INTRODUCTION

After graduating from college two of my best hometown buddies had joined the volunteer fire department in the town where we all grew up. Boys of my generation had fantasies of becoming professional athletes, movie stars, police officers, soldiers, or firefighters. We dreamed of becoming famous or heroic. GI Joe boys we were!

I could not resist the temptation to live out a childhood desire to be a firefighter. At the time I was student teaching and trained to become a Reserve Firefighter for the city of San Clemente in Southern California. Technically it was a volunteer role, but we were paid a small stipend each time we responded to a fire alarm. It was a rewarding experience and I considered it a possible career track if I did not stick with teaching.

Meanwhile, I was volunteering as a youth worker at my church and the youth pastor, Ken, was a major influence in my life. After a year and a half of being a Reserve Firefighter and a semester into paramedic training, Ken asked me to join him in a move up to Oregon to start a teen wilderness adventure camp. For several summers before we had organized camping and water-skiing trips for our own youth group, but Ken now wanted to take it a step further and start his own camping ministry.

I agonized over the decision but felt like it was an opportunity and a calling I could not pass up. Being a firefighter had left a deep mark upon me, but I felt a calling from God to outdoor ministry. I packed my bags and left San Clemente and moved to Portland with Ken and his family.

The next three years were vigorous and electrifying. We established Creative Camping Ministries and organized dozens of summer outdoor wilderness camps for youth groups throughout the region. During the school year I taught junior high school at a public school while we would lead several weekend retreats during the year for various church groups.

I will always look back on this experience with fond memories. Our camps coaxed teenagers out of their everyday routine and preoccupations, unplugged them from all their devices, and created an atmosphere where we formed meaningful relationships and had conversations about life that truly mattered. Setting up camp, cooking on an open fire, water skiing, competitions, skits, impactful speakers, and sharing, forged bonds and changed lives.

But after three years it became increasingly difficult to raise the financial resources to keep the operation viable. We had little choice; it was not possible to continue. We celebrated our victories, lamented our stalemate, and began considering what was next in our lives.

The gratification of being a spiritual influence in the lives of these teenagers compelled me to seriously consider going into full-time ministry. I decided to pursue a Master of Divinity degree at Fuller Seminary back in Southern California. Upon graduating I was offered the Youth Pastor position at Peninsula Bible Church in Palo Alto where I cut my teeth in ministry. The church was known for teaching "New Covenant" theology, which emphasizes the love, grace and empowerment of God as the framework for living the Christian life, as opposed to "Old Covenant" mindset that stipulates that obedience to religious rules, rites and regulations are necessary to remain in good standing with God.

I have seen too many Christians, including myself, living according to the Old Covenant mentality—a performance-based relationship with God, constantly striving to earn and maintain God's approval and blessing. Jesus invited people weary of religion to come to him for rest, replenishment and renewal, and yet our churches are filled with people who feel exhausted, self-contempt and emptiness inside. Though Jesus said that following him would show one how to live freely and lightly, people in the pew often feel weighed down and shackled by their Churchianity. Many of them eventually leave church and their faith altogether.

My years as Youth Pastor at Peninsula Bible Church laid the spiritual foundation for my grace-based relationship with God and my approach to ministry as a pastor. I learned to walk in that freedom, security and lightness of spirit Jesus spoke of and saw my ministry as inviting others into that same life. It was at Peninsula that I met Heidi, married, and started a family. In a few short years we became a family of four. To this day I am partial toward the gratification and gravity of ministry to adolescents and teens. I also realized it was not realistic to provide for my growing family on a youth pastor salary.

After nearly a decade in Palo Alto I accepted a call to serve a church in Austin, Texas as Associate Pastor. Over the years I held a special place in my heart for first responders. I would remember my dream to become a firefighter and felt regret on occasion that I had not persisted on that path. But low and behold at my church in Austin I discovered that several men were volunteer firefighters. After a number of months of recruiting me, I was convinced to join them at the CE-Bar Volunteer Fire Department, Travis County Fire District #12.

Soon after joining I proposed to the fire chief, Buddy, that we needed a chaplain. It is no secret that firefighters have a dangerous job. They often help people on the worst day of their life. The scenarios can sometimes be gruesome and involve loss of life. During my service as a volunteer firefighter in Austin, there was a fire where two children died. The emotional toll it takes is intense. As you can imagine with any fire department, over time, there are seriously injured or line of duty deaths which impact firefighter families. I discussed with Buddy that I would be willing to be a "pastor" to our fire department, offering support, grief counseling, and to be someone that our firefighters could talk to when they were struggling. I became the department's first chaplain.

Completing my Emergency Medical Technician training, I spent nearly eight years in Austin responding to fires and emergency medical calls as a firefighter, EMT, and chaplain. I quickly learned that the need for a fire and first responder chaplain was not only to offer support, comfort and counseling to personnel and their families, but to civilians on the scene where there is tragedy and death. Church pastor by day, firefighter and first responder by night; whether it was teaching behind a pulpit in church or hanging off the back of a fire engine speeding to a fire, it was all God's work to me. Over the years, I responded to countless emergencies involving tragedy and suffering as a chaplain, as well as a few close calls myself, escaping death in the line of duty fighting fires.

My years in Austin were some of the best of my life and our family continued to grow, Heidi giving birth to our third child. I knew the next step in my ministerial career was to be a Senior Pastor, and that opportunity came back in California. I was contacted about the Senior Pastor position of a church community in the East Bay of San Francisco. After a couple visits, they made an offer. I accepted. It did not take long for me to jump into the world of chaplaincy once again. I joined the ranks as a volunteer chaplain in our local East Bay fire district and county sheriff's office. This immersed me in the world of law enforcement chaplaincy work. I was trained in Critical Incident Stress Debriefing (CISD), designed to minimize the impact of a traumatic event and to aid in psychological and emotional recovery for law enforcement professionals. The spectrum of duties for a law enforcement chaplain include law enforcement family support, death notifications, community care, and various responsibilities including possible hostage negotiation situations.

It was not lost on me that I was straddling two vocational tracks, a ministerial career and chaplaincy work, which progressively became more difficult to juggle. The church board noticed this as well, and occasionally we discussed it and a few of them expressed concern. After six years of serving the church I was asked to choose. Though I loved the people and had given the best of me in being their pastor, my heart was in the chaplaincy work. Many years prior I had walked away from my dream to be a fulltime firefighter to become a minister. But the work of a first responder chaplain would allow me to do both.

The church board and I agreed that it was the best choice for me and the church. Resigning as a church pastor, even in the best of situations, is painful and difficult. I felt tremendous stress. Yes, I wanted to pursue chaplaincy work, but it was not like I had a job waiting for me. Most chaplain positions are volunteer roles and seldom paid. Meanwhile, I still had a mortgage and a family of five to provide for.

There were some bleak and disheartening days as we struggled to determine what was next. I experienced a deep depression and saw no path forward. There is not an abundance of jobs for a guy with a seminary degree who needs to generate enough income for a family of five, not to mention the matter of health insurance. What I most wanted to do was continue pursuing my chaplaincy work, but it would not provide an income or benefits. I felt hopelessly stuck. You might say this was my "dark night of the soul," in which I wrestled with God about what seemed to be an impossible predicament and the uncertainty of our future.

19

When trials and hardships come into our lives, we often feel desperation and wish for divine or miraculous intervention to rescue us out of it. But I have often found that God's grace includes finding our way forward through more common means. For me it began with the unwavering support and confidence of my wife. We also had some close and devoted friends who walked with us through this season of turbulent transition. I cleared my head and began wondering about the possibility of starting a non-profit agency through which I could receive financial support for my role as a chaplain in the community. Turns out, a friend of mine knew someone in Southern California who several years earlier had done exactly that—he had started a non-profit organization to serve a police and fire department as a chaplain.

My friend put me in touch with him and we immediately hit it off. He offered to allow me to use his non-profit to initially raise supporters. That was my path forward. Over a hundred people I contacted throughout the US including Portland, San Francisco Bay Area, Austin, and Southern California were eager to support my work as a chaplain, and they recruited others to do the same. All this came together just three months after resigning as pastor of the church. If that does not qualify as "divine intervention," I am not sure what does. That network of supporters has grown and continued to this day.

We often hear how "God works in mysterious ways" but it also comes in very ordinary ways—an unwavering spouse, caring friends, an unexpected development, and the willingness to break out of your comfort zone to actualize a new possibility. Sometimes we are on the receiving end of these small graces and godsends; sometimes we are these to others.

Working alongside police officers, firefighters, and paramedics, as a first responder chaplain now for over 20 years, I have often found myself thrust into people's worst possible nightmares and tragedies. My hope is always, in some way, to be a grace or godsend in moments of catastrophic despair and suffering. However, like all first responders, this work takes a heavy toll. I was not prepared to witness such anguish and heartache when I first began my work as a chaplain back in 1998. I had no idea what I was getting into like most cops and firefighters who enter their careers with a noble aspiration to serve the community but along the way encounter evil, murder, suicide, tragedy, carnage and lives destroyed by drugs, alcohol and crime.

During this journey something greater than the mark of sorrow, grief and dismay this work leaves upon you, has happened inside me. My faith has been challenged, confronted, tested, defied, gutted, ransacked, pushed to the brink, and turned upside down; only to become more real, more human, more durable, more whole, more courageous, more hopeful, more loving and more liberating.

I want to show you how all that happened. Let us take a ride. I want you to come with me on the actual scenes of my work as a first responder chaplain. You need to see what I saw, hear what I heard, feel what I felt, cry like I cried, doubt where I doubted, believe where I believed, and hope where I found hope. You cannot exactly experience what I did, I know, but I can bring you into my experiences as a chaplain where we share similar struggles of doubt, heartache, unbelief, and the search for hope and meaning in a world of hardship and suffering. As a warning, this journey is not for the faint of heart.

Etched on my memory is the occasion when an officer and I had to give a death notification to the parents of a seventeen-year-old boy who lived only a few blocks away. The boy was tragically killed on impact in a single car accident a mile from his home. He was the same age and a school mate of my daughter, both of whom were to start their senior year of high school the next morning.

I met the officer at the hospital where the body had been transported. Without knowing any specifics about the fatality, the officer and I entered the room where this boy was laying on a gurney. He had been cleaned up and a sheet covered him up to his shoulders. I took one look at his face and immediately recognized him. It was dear, sweet Robert who lived around the corner from us. The same Robert I watched as a little boy, play in the park next to our house. The same Robert who walked to middle school with my daughter. The same Robert who religiously practiced free throws in his driveway with his dad.

Grief-stricken, I muttered to the officer that I knew this boy. Now we had to go to his home and inform his parents what every mother and father hopes they never have to hear. A sick feeling of despair sank to the pit of my stomach as it began to dawn on me how the whole community would be devastated.

Officer Rollins and I drove to Robert's home around 9:30 pm–a warm August night on the eve of the boy's high school senior year. The short ten-minute drive to their home was hell. There are dark moments when a chaplain can feel deep-seated doubt and disbelief–questioning that you chose this work, doubting that it makes any difference, shaken that such cruel tragedies happen, and disbelief that a good and all-powerful God would find this okay. I could not stand the thought of breaking this heartbreaking news to the mother and father. A sense of panic was setting in. My wife, only a block away from Robert's home, had gone to bed early because of a busy morning. Being a warm evening, she had all the bedroom windows open.

Pulling up to the home, the parents saw our patrol car through their living room window and raced outside, having spent the last hour distressed by their son not returning home. Mom and dad were frantic, and hysteria set in before we could say a word. They demanded to know what happened and refused to go back into the house as we first suggested.

Standing in their front yard on this warm August night I told them that their son was killed. It was unbearable to see their reaction. I sometimes still hear the mother's screams in nightmares that jar me awake at night. She wailed so violently that my wife at home, in bed, a block away was startled from her sleep. They were screams the entire neighborhood heard. Inside I was undone by the despair and heartache I was witnessing.

Later in the evening, officer Rollins, who also had a teenager daughter, told me that for the first time in his 15-year career he almost threw up from the emotional trauma of seeing these two parents reacting to the tragic news. Most people are sensitized to tragedy and death, which are the top headlines and trending stories, and depicted countless times in films and television. But what gets lost on a screen is the humanity of the moment when people's hearts and lives are shattered by the unbearable loss of someone they love deeply. Words cannot describe the feelings of heartrending anguish people experience at times of significant loss.

Being up close and personal to so many horrific and gruesome tragedies has been costly. Throughout the years I have consulted therapists about having symptoms of PTSD. Intrusive memories, trouble sleeping, emotional numbness, depression, feelings of guilt–these are some of the realities I, and virtually all first responders, experience. Rather than shoving down the volatility of emotions first responders feel, it is critical they have an outlet to share their stories, express their thoughts and feelings and process their traumatic experiences. Writing this book, which has involved reliving many harrowing occasions, was not always easy. But telling these stories and sharing my heart have been cathartic and therapeutic.

You might be wondering how God fits into all this. My faith and relationship with God have not protected me from the suffering, sorrow, and heartache of the human experience. It did not protect Jesus either. Jesus himself tasted the depths of mental anguish, emotional distress, and physical trauma in ways few of us every will. He also met others in their suffering. Jesus did not theologize people's losses and tragedies, he entered into it in a spirit of solidarity, empathy, compassion, and love. In one of the most poignant episodes in the Bible when Jesus arrives on the scene of another's heartache and grief, his response is described in two words: "Jesus wept."

In my view, Jesus is a model for the work and ministry of a first responder chaplain. He did not come to people as the fix-it guy and answer man. He did not cite bible verses or hold a prayer service. Jesus simply came alongside people in their suffering and offered himself– his presence and understanding, his tenderness and humanity, his mercy and solidarity. There is something between living in denial and being swallowed whole by the pain and suffering of human existence, and Jesus lived there. I understand now that my calling as a first responder chaplain is learning to live there, as Jesus did.

The subject of God, almost, always comes up in the midst and aftermath of a tragic event. Over the years there are two things that have stood out to me, which ultimately led to my writing this book. The first is how much people need a power greater than themselves to face the volatile, distressing, and agonizing realities of human existence. Sometimes life is too much. Our tribulations eclipse our ability to cope, feel hope, bounce back and overcome life's misfortunes, calamities, heartbreaks, and sorrows. In our darkest, weakest and most vulnerable moments in life when we feel pillaged and powerless, we need help from a transcendent and trustworthy source that will see us through.

What has secondly stood out to me, is how many people doubt that the God they learned in church would qualify for the job. The title of this book, *Used to Go to Church*, is based upon the countless times that people have responded to my inquiry about their faith with, "I used to go to church." Through further inquiry I would learn that their former church experience left them in a spiritual no-man's-land.

On the one hand, they did not want to write off God categorically. But on the other hand, the "God" they learned in church seemed irrelevant, arcane, exacting, beyond belief, and even absurd. There is no shortage of people in the world like this, maybe you are one of them.

I understand. During those years when I was juggling being a pastor and a community chaplain, I began feeling cognitive dissonance between the theological answers I confidently proclaimed at church, and the unanswerable suffering I was thrust into each time I was dispatched to a traumatic scene. Too often my theological and doctrnal explanations did not seem to add up to much in the face of tragic loss.

My conception of God and faith has been recast in the crucible of human hardship. This book is that story. G. K. Chesterton wrote, "The Christian ideal has not been tried and found wanting; it's been found difficult and left untried." True faith is not belief in God *in spite of* life's tragedies and the weighty questions they evoke for which we do not have good answers. Rather, true faith is knowing that it is precisely at our darkest and most tragic moments, that there *is* something greater than ourselves.

A "God" proclaimed to be powerful in worship songs and church sermons but helpless or absent in the carnage of human suffering is no God at all. True faith is not the absence of doubt; it is not suppressing the normal volatility of emotions we feel in the face of loss; it is not a religious stoicism that hides behind bible verses and pat theological answers. True faith does not even rule out feeling forgotten and abandoned, even by God. Jesus felt all the above. True faith is knowing that there *is* something greater than ourselves, even greater than all our doubts, disbelief, and feelings in those moments.

I have been given the gift of several friends whom I have known since childhood, which I count as one of my life's greatest treasures. One of those friends, Jeff, is truly closer than a brother. Early in the writing of this book, I asked Jeff to critique the first few draft chapters I had completed. He gladly agreed and a few days later he sent me an email with his feedback.

In his email, he wrote that the chapters were "a little too real for me." Jeff's middle son of three boys tragically took his own life in 2012 at the age of 20. As you might imagine, he and his wife Karon suffered many dark moments of grief and heartache. Losing a child to suicide is perhaps the most devastating loss a person could endure. Reading my chapters gave voice to the struggle he has had in trying to make peace with the death of his son, and square it with his belief in God.

Jeff shared in his email that the people who would most be drawn to my book are those desperate for something that I will not be able to offer—an answer to their suffering. Answers to questions like: Why? Why me? Why this? He wrote, "No one wants to get to the end of a book only to hear the same old reply common from most Christians… 'in the end, I don't know why we suffer', or something along those lines."

He continued, "The difficult part is, once you have described all these horrific circumstances, how are you going to answer the unanswerable? This, to me, is the challenge you face in authoring a book like this. If there is no 'answer' to all the tragedy you describe, how will you ever hope to encourage folks to have faith in God? I realize that you have a whole lot more to write but I would encourage you to try and steer away early on in the book from implying that you are leading up to an 'answer' about suffering. For me, God never explained my loss and still has not. I waited for Him and I demanded an explanation for a long time. It still has not come. I realize now it never will."

Jeff was right. I do not have all the answers. It is a difficult pill to swallow for a guy with an MDiv and the former pastor who never met a problem I could not explain with proper theology, carefully exegeted from the original Hebrew or Greek. I took to heart the advice he offered. As Jeff warned, you will be disappointed if you are expecting airtight theological answers to the many heartrending questions that any reasonable person would ask about God in the face of catastrophic loss, bottomless grief, and a heart torn in two. It was not my aim to write such a book. Many such books attempting this feat have already been written. Heck, if C.S. Lewis in *The Problem Pain* did not explain suffering suitably, I surely cannot.

This book is not about me trying to explain suffering. What you are about to read is my story. It is my story of coming to terms with God and faith in moments and situations ripe for doubt and unbelief. The last several years my spiritual growth has not been the byproduct of bible studies, prayer services and accountability groups, but from what I have experienced and learned at the scenes of life's most out of the box circumstances.

In his email, Jeff reminded me that I led the memorial service for his son, JV. In my remarks, I did not try to explain the death of his son, put some theological spin on it, or even soften the blow of its impact on Jeff and Karon, and the entire community. There are no tidy homilies for a young person who takes their own life. What I most remember about my words was squarely facing the sorrow and heartache of this tragic loss, and an appeal to all in attendance to earnestly be expressions of love, grace, tenderheartedness, support and hope to one another. Jeff said that my words that day did not dispel the anguish and heartache of the tragic loss of his son, but they sparked a flicker of hope that there was something beyond, something deeper, something greater than his unanswered questions and suffering. God is either love, or He is not.

Rosanne Cash wrote, "Loss is the great unifier, the terrible club to which we all eventually belong." Maybe you purchased this book because you are seeking peace and healing from your own loss, grief, and sorrow. Perhaps you are a firefighter, police officer or paramedic who shows up every day to scenes of trauma, death and devastation. Maybe you have lost faith in God because of your own heartbreaks and tragedies, or the human suffering and carnage you see strewn across each morning's news headlines. You may be someone who could not accept the God you found in church, or perhaps you were even deeply damaged and wounded by your involvement in organized religion. Whatever compelled you to pick up this book, I hope my story stirs new faith that you are not alone, that suffering does not render the human journey meaningless, and that there is something greater than any inventive theological explanation could provide.

CHAPTER 1

DOES GOD MATTER?

In the time it takes to drive from our house to the gym where I work out, about ten minutes, there is one suicide in the US. I am guessing most people are not thinking this as they drive to the gym. I do. Some of the most heartbreaking situations I have walked into as a first responder chaplain have been suicides. Like 3912 Acklen Drive, on September 14th at 1:27 pm.

Thirty minutes before I arrived, a father found his twenty-year-old son hanging in the garage. He cut him down, called 911 and started CPR. Suicide is the second leading cause of death for those 15-24 in age.

I pulled up in front of the house and before exiting my car, noticed what a nice upper middle-class neighborhood I was in. After days of rain, it was a gorgeous day–blue skies, warmth of the mid-day sun, and cleansed air. A person would feel invigorated on a day like this. But tragedies can happen on any day, even sunny and exquisite days. I was sitting in front of a house which behind the front door was a family's most harrowing nightmare.

When my phone rang twenty minutes earlier, and saw it was our police dispatch calling, I knew there was a fatality involved but had no further details. My heart always sinks knowing there is a death. A police dispatch call almost always means a sudden or tragic death. In a sense, every death is a tragic death, sudden or not, expected or untimely. But what happened at 3912 Acklen Drive is the kind of death that loved ones never recover from. It is the kind of death that would make a person lose faith in everything, including and especially God.

A police officer on the scene walked over to my car to inform me of the details. Inside the home there were three individuals, a 20-year-old boy who had hung himself, his father who dialed 911 after finding him, and the boy's younger sister.

Making my way to the front door, I felt overwhelmed by the magnitude of despair I knew was inside, and the inconceivable task of somehow offering something meaningful. As a first responder chaplain, there is a sense in which you know that you will fail in every situation. In times of deep suffering what people want, you are not capable of giving. What do they want? For it all to go away. The Breton Fisherman's Prayer, which I have on a plaque, is the best chaplain's prayer I know, "O God, the sea is so great, and my boat is so small."

Standing on the front porch, I am conflicted. Part of me wants to turn back around, submit my resignation as a chaplain, be done, and never have to do this again. But another part of me knows this is not just a job, it is a calling. Deep down I know that walking through that front door is why I am here in this world. Some days a blessing and other days a curse–my life's work is being an expression of solace, solidarity, and support in the moments of another human being's greatest tragedy.

All first responders have a specific role to play at a heartrending scene like this—patrol officers, firefighters, paramedics, and coroner. As a police and fire chaplain, my role is to offer comfort and guide them through the first few hours of shock and grief. Most people equate the term 'chaplain' with some form of clergy person. They see you as a representative of God, which means you either have answers or faith that you can impart to them to help mitigate their pain.

To be honest, after 20 years of responding to calls such as this one, I have discovered that my own faith has been shaken and I have been forced to reconsider what faith really means. I know that there are few, if any words, that will alleviate the anguish of a father who just found his son's lifeless body hanging from a rope. I wonder to myself if God is going to really matter here today. How's that for the steadfast and unflinching ambassador of the Most High???

After a couple knocks, the front door slowly opened and before me stood a distraught middle-aged man of slight build. There is something almost sacred about that moment when you first encounter another human being in their suffering. He could barely lift his head to make eye contact but when he did, he visually noted the embroidered police badge on my polo shirt. As I stepped inside, he then caught the word 'Chaplain' also embroidered on my shirt, which he spoke aloud, and then stuttering in a weak and trembling voice said, "We need a clergy person."

He quickly asked, "Can we do last rites?" Last rites are prayers and pastoral words given shortly before death, but not for the already deceased. But this is not the time to quibble over sacraments. Just thirty minutes ago, this father found his twenty-year-old son hanging from a noose in their garage.

Upon discovering his son, the father cut him down, called 911 and started CPR. There are few images in a man's life, if any, which could be more tortuous than your young son's lifeless body hanging before you. There is no delete option for that mental photograph which will haunt this father for the remainder of his life.

He was too late to stop or rescue his son, and the boy was well past the point of being revived. The paramedics who arrived on scene at once pronounced him deceased. These are the worst kind of calls for firefighters and paramedics who are wired and trained to rescue people and save lives. When they come to a scene like this where nothing can be done, they feel powerless and can even take it as a failure.

First responders, many being mothers and fathers themselves, always feel a primal emotional attachment with parents who lose children. This was clearly the case in this traumatic death in which the father was hemorrhaging with hysteria and inconsolable grief. The police officers and firefighters quickly realized that a chaplain was needed.

The officers remained on scene to carry out an investigation while the firefighters and paramedics were packing up to leave. Departing a scene like this is vexing for every first responder. You just do not walk away, unaffected. Some first responders wish they could stay and comfort the loved ones. I have seen many firefighters and officers who are very chaplain-like on scenes such as this. Others cannot escape fast enough—not because they do not care, but because they care too much. They can't bear watching the suffering of the loved ones who remain among the living. Most won't admit or even realize a bite has been taken out of their soul.

Like some of my comrades, I showed up that day not only as a first responder but as a dad. When I learned there was a twenty-year-old who committed suicide at his parent's home, I was reticent to respond. I had a twenty-year-old son at home on winter break from college who had been struggling with anxiety and depression his first semester away. I have never declined to go on a call but for the first time, I seriously considered it when the dispatcher informed me, we had a 10-56 (the ten-code for suicide) involving a 20-year-old male.

After a few minutes assessing the situation I asked one of our officers to dispatch one of our female chaplains to the scene to tend to the young man's eighteen-year-old sister at home taking all this in. Looking back I needed a collegue to be a source of strength for me too. The mother had been notified as she was driving out of town to visit a relative, and instantly turned around. I could not imagine that drive home, carrying the heartbreaking news that her son was dead.

The paramedics had left, and several officers were still on the scene, one of them relaying information to the county coroner who was on his way. The father was pacing back and forth talking to himself in a state of emotional trauma, and uncertain about what to do next. I offered to pray over the young man in lieu of last rites, and he asked if we could wait until the mother arrived.

One of the first ways I engage with a person as a chaplain, where the death of a loved one is involved, is to initiate a simple conversation. Acute emotional trauma can quickly spiral, and gently drawing the person into a connection helps stabilize them so they can survive and cope the brunt of shock that hits them.

Since he had mentioned "last rites," I assumed he must be a religious person, most likely Catholic. After expressing my condolences and intent to support him, I asked if he was Catholic. He responded, "Yes, but we don't attend church anymore."

Over the years of my service as a chaplain, if I have heard that response once, I've heard it a thousand times when inquiring about a person's faith or religious affiliation. It does not leave you with much to decipher about where they stand with respect to their belief in God. The world is filled with church leavers–people who stop attending church or are no longer actively involved in organized religion. Some of them abandon belief in God altogether, most pursue spirituality on different terms. There is a growing number of people who identify themselves as "spiritual but not religious" and also those who speak of a Christ-centered spirituality but who do not attend church.

What a person believes about God in moments of despair and deep human suffering, matters. It matters in terms of whether you believe there is a power greater than yourself to strengthen you in times of fragility, exhaustion, and collapse. It matters as a basis for hope in the face of devastating loss, and the assurance there is meaning to life that transcends human tragedy.

What a person believes about God matters with respect to how one understands death and what happens after you die. It matters with regard to believing that there is a pathway one can follow to withstand tragedy, overcome hardship, grieve loss, and heal from heartache. Beliefs about God can be the difference between someone feeling alone and abandoned in an impersonal and random universe that is callously grinding forward, or feeling a connection with everything in existence, characterized by deep feelings of love and destiny.

I had no idea what this father believed about God. My experience with the countless people who have told me they "used to go to church" is that they do not entirely know. Typically, the fact that they left church means that the God they learned there did not add up or square with real life and did not make any real difference in their lives. For many people, the idea of God does not appear on their radar again until hardship or tragedy strikes, like that fateful day at 3912 Acklen Drive.

As the father opened up, he shared that his son had dropped out of college due to anxiety and depression. Just months before this boy's suicide, my own son nearly dropped the same university for similar reasons. I also learned that this young man's sister was also a classmate of my son at this college. I learned that this young man was a gamer who played online video games at night and slept during the day. In my own home I struggled with the same issues regarding my son. Often when I am at a heartrending scene as a first responder chaplain I am thinking, this could be me: my tragedy, my loss, my heartache, and in this case, my son.

When the mother arrived, another tidal wave of grief erupted. Mom, dad, and daughter embraced and wept a sorrow so tortuous that it required steely resolve not to lose it myself.

The father asked if I would pray over his son, who was laying on the garage floor with a yellow ground cloth draped over his lifeless body, revealing only his face. We all gathered around his body, while three police officers and the deputy coroner looked on.

As a chaplain, most people are expecting that I will somehow interject religion into the circumstances. Every situation is different, but the goal is never to shoehorn God into a tragic scene. I see my role as being a human expression of God's comfort, empathy, caring and love. That was the whole point of Jesus, wasn't it? He was called "Immanuel" meaning, "God with us." My calling as a chaplain is to embody that truth at every scene of suffering—God is not in heaven or the neverlands of the universe observing from a distance; God is present, God is real, God matters—right here and right now.

I knelt at the head of their boy and for a few moments studied his face. I was not going to rush this precious sacred moment. Then I made eye contact with mom and dad and said that their request to pray over their son implied to me they had some belief in God. I shared that my particular belief was that we are never separated from God–not in our darkest moments of suffering or even in death.

This is why God matters.

I looked back down at the boy and placed one of my hands on his forehead. In that moment, I was not just Nick the chaplain. I was Nick the father. I was not just Nick, the clergyman encouraging faith. I was Nick, the human being who needed faith. I was not just a witness to the tears of grief of others, I was shedding them myself. Did God matter to Nick?

In a garage, at 3912 Acklen Drive, a heartsick family, three police officers and a coroner–that was church. No pulpit or PowerPoint, no band or multi-media, no bells and spells, no lectionary or liturgy, no icons or incense, but real church.

One of the most significant existential questions is: Does God exist? My question is a bit more practical: Does God matter? Many people are hesitant to conclusively say there is no God, but they do not have a good answer to the "So What" question. So what, if God exists? They went to church, they practiced religion, they listened to sermons, they gave their money, they read their Bible, but for what?

More and more people are skeptical of what that learned about God in church. They wonder: Did God really ask Abraham to kill his own son as a sign of devotion? Would God command genocidal warfare in order to secure his honor? Will God always protect and prosper those who obey the Bible's commandments? Would a loving God really condemn the bulk of the human race to eternal conscious torment in hell?

Too often God matters to people because they fear God or they are striving to earn God's favor through their religious devotion. Is that the deal? Does God only matter because he punches your ticket to heaven or because he knows who's been naughty or nice, and blesses them accordingly?

But why is it in moments of tragedy, heartache, and loss that a person who has not given much thought to God for years will suddenly become cognizant of God? This father left church years ago and yet the first thing that came to his mind when we interacted was his desire for me to pray over his son.

In life's bleakest moments, we long to know there is something greater than ourselves—greater than our sorrow, greater than our loss, greater than our heartbreak, greater than our suffering. Sadness, grief, pain, and anguish is one way our deepest awareness signals to us that our experience of reality is not yet complete.

Where there is darkness, we long for light. When we are broken, we cry out for healing. In our despair, we search for hope. When we buckle in heartache to our knees, we need a reason to get back up. In those moments when what we love most is ripped away from us, we want to believe there is still a reason to go on.

This is why God matters. God is the completion of the incompletion of life, which we most feel as human beings in moments of suffering. There are many different beliefs, conceptions, understandings, theories, teachings about who and what God is. But one thing everyone agrees on: if God exists, God is whole, absolute, complete, illimitable, unconfined, all-encompassing, and infinite.

God matters because life is not complete without God. I do not necessarily mean the "God" many people learned in church. I mean God as the ultimate and highest reality in the universe—the alpha and omega, the first word and the last word, the now and the not yet, the imminent and the transcendent. This description is not some poetic theological statement for a Sunday sermon. It is the basis for having peace, joy, hope, strength, faith, courage, meaning, well-being, and contentment in a world of tragedy, heartache, sadness, and suffering.

God matters because without God you are only living half of life. The light in the darkness, healing in our brokenness, hope in our despair, and our reason to get back up and go on, is based upon something we know intuitively deep within us—there is something more, something greater, something beyond the hardship of the moment.

When life is going well, we are less aware of the incomplete reality of our lives and feel little need for help. But when tragedy strikes, we are painfully confronted by the unpredictability, fragility, and cruelties of the human experience. Those are the moments we feel a need for something greater than ourselves. As a first responder chaplain, I feel my greatest contribution is to represent and be an expression of the light, hope, strength, and faith that is always available to every human being, even if their pain and suffering in the moment blinds them to it.

The coroner determines the circumstances, manner, and cause of sudden deaths where an attending physician is not able to ascertain this information. A coroner also makes an inquiry and does an autopsy in cases of deaths resulting from homicide, suicide, certain accidents, and when deaths are unattended. Once the forensic examination of the body is completed by the coroner, a family has 72-hours to arrange to have the body transported.

This was the next conversation I had with the mother and father at the scene. Part of my role as a chaplain is to compassionately inform and aid people in addressing the necessary practical matters in tragic circumstances. I explained to them the process and helped them make arrangements. I always leave my card and let people know I am someone they can call for support. I give them materials about additional mental health resources such as grief counseling, and contact information for funeral details.

But even with all that, I am always conflicted when it is time for me to leave a scene as traumatic as this. In the car drive home, I found myself in the same spot where I began. Did I make a difference? Was it enough? Will this family get through this? How does one ever recover from the suicide of their child? "O God, the sea is so great and my boat is so small."

Then the thought occurred to me. If God matters because God makes all things complete, then I can have faith and confidence in something greater than myself at that scene. Not just that scene, but every scene. And not just the hardships, tragedies, and suffering of others, but my own. Not just at 3912 Acklen Drive, but at my home and life. Not just that dad, but this dad. And not just me, but you.

And even as long and difficult a road it will be for this family as they process their loss, heartache and grief, there will be something greater still.

There will be the rest of the story.

The complete story. The God one.

CHAPTER 2

WITHOUT A TRACE

Last year there were 424,066 cases of missing children in the US. In my state of California, we have the second highest number of Amber alerts. Missing children cases are sometimes runaways, others are abductions or kidnappings. Some have happy endings, some do not. Some children are found and returned home; others vanish without a trace.

One evening while under the sink, failing to unclog our garbage disposal, my phone on the counter began buzzing. I called Heidi to hand me my phone, it was my friend Rick. In a voice of desperation, he explained he was at Don's home, a mutual friend, because Don's 15-year-old daughter was missing. She had gone to school that morning like any other day, but never returned home. Rick urged me to come over.

The first 48 hours after a child has gone missing are the most critical for a case, and every minute is agonizing for the parents who wait in fear and helplessness. I threw on my chaplain uniform and headed out.

DAY ONE

I was acquainted with Don and his family. They lived just five minutes from our home. Years ago, our two youngest boys had played on the same soccer team when I was head coach. Don volunteered to be my assistant, and we enjoyed a fun season with our sons. We did not see each other much after that, except the occasional coming and going of dropping off or picking up the boys from one another's home.

Don's oldest daughter, Annie, who was 15, had not returned home from school that afternoon. Annie was a classmate of my daughter, born in the same hospital, four days apart. There are pros and cons to being a chaplain on scenes where you personally know the people involved. On the one hand, it is helpful because there's trust and rapport already established. The challenge lies in the difficulty of letting these traumatic scenarios go when you personally know the people affected.

Already gathered at the home was a large contingent of the county Sheriff's search and rescue team who were assembling and staging in preparation to begin a neighborhood search. Our search and rescue team is the largest and one of the best trained in the state of California. They are often called upon to assist in searches all over the region.

As a part of my chaplain role, it is common for me to be called upon to meet the search and rescue team when they return from a search after discovering a deceased victim. I joined the team after the Tubbs Fire of 2017, at the time, the most destructive wildfire in California history. The fire burned 36,810 acres and 22 people were killed in Sonoma County by the fire. We went through hundreds of burned down homes searching for any sign of human remains.

Search and rescue teams always have high hopes to find their missing subject alive and for some it is devastating to have the search result in death. Every missing person case is top priority but when it involves a child it is all hands on deck.

When I arrived, there was a throng of people gathered in and around the home. Numerous law enforcement officers were present, including the town police chief who came to show his support. Other family members and close friends had come to sit with the family. I had to navigate my way through the front yard and made my way inside the house, and found Don and his wife, Joan, in the kitchen talking to the Incident Commander of the search and rescue team.

These conversations with law enforcement officers can be agonizing as they try to determine if the missing person is a victim of foul play, injured or suffering a medical emergency, or a runaway. The necessary questions asked of parents of a missing child can be torturing. Few parents will believe their child would run away.

We all had high hopes that Don's little girl, Annie, would be found. The first decision is establishing a search area. This is typically a circle based on the last place the missing person was seen, which in this case was Annie's school. As the search progresses, that point will change—for example, if an article of clothing is found along a trail. A hasty search team is typically the first to be deployed. Their job is to pair up and move quickly. The goal is to scan high-probability areas and end the search as soon as possible. Time is of the essence with missing children.

Behind the initial search team, a grid search team moves slower and more methodically, combing the area with a long line of volunteers. Grid searchers typically find clues that help more experienced professionals find the missing person.

As each minute passed, Don and Joan became more distressed. There is no chaplain manual that tells you what to do in a missing persons case, or any tragic situation for that matter. There are basic chaplain guidelines and best practices, but in the end, you are on your own when you are at a scene. You rely upon your experience, discernment, and intuition.

My initial mindset with Don and Joan was to be a stabilizing presence, which was easier to achieve because we already knew each other personally. For parents with a missing child, hanging on to your sanity one minute at a time is a tall order. Often it involves irrational thoughts. Parents of missing children are prone to blame themselves. You never know the timeline for a search and rescue operation. They can be days, even weeks or longer.

A ground team of close to 100 search and rescue professionals and volunteers were canvassing the area where Annie had been last seen. The first hours of any incident are often stressful and confusing. The information is often vague, incomplete, and often contradictory. Initial updates about Annie indicated there had been no leads or clues found. Each update was a devastating blow to Don and Joan. For the parents of a missing child, every excruciating minute feels like an eternity. The hourly chime of their wall clock felt ominous.

The late-night hours surrendered to the sunrise, and there was no Annie.

DAY TWO

By the next morning, the Bay Area news media had picked up the story, and all the San Francisco area news stations were putting up pictures of this sweet pony-tailed 15-year-old girl from Danville who was missing. A hotline number was set up for anyone who might have any relevant information. A Missing Person Flyer was widely posted in the Bay Area and public places in and around the search area.

After the report of a missing person is taken, the subject of the search is entered into the National Crime Information Center computer, which gives law enforcement professionals access to investigative databases to gather important information about the search subject such as cell phone location information, social media accounts, and surveillance camera footage. A Child Is Missing, Inc. (ACIM) is a non-profit organization, which has a missing child alert program and recovery center that assists law enforcement agencies nationwide in the early search and recovery of missing children.

Don and Joan's emotional strain became more unbearable as each hour passed. They had been without sleep or food for eighteen hours straight. I encouraged them to eat and at least take a nap in order to maintain their strength. With the promise that they would immediately be informed if any new developments were reported, they agreed. They decided to take turns, Joan would nap first while Don ate and then Joan would eat and Don sleep. I decided to go home myself, at least for a few hours.

It was near impossible to sleep, thinking about Annie. Parents know of the sick panicked feeling you get when you lose a child somewhere even if just for a few minutes. I will never forget a vacation trip when we were shopping at a gift store up in the Sierra mountains. Our three children at the time were young, including Trevor, our 2-year-old. Heidi and I wandered around the store with Heidi's mother while we left Trevor with his 6-year-old sister and 8-year-old brother in a small designated play area inside the store.

After about ten minutes we were ready to leave and when we went back to the play area Trevor was gone. His siblings had no clue where he went. It was not a big scare initially until we discovered he was not inside the store. Heidi was on the verge of panic mode, and I ran out of the door and began searching all the stores up and down the strip mall. No Trevor, and no one said they had seen a toddler wandering around. I scanned the parking lot, and just at that moment I saw an old creepy white van pulling out of a parking space and speeding off. Have you ever noticed it is always a white van?!

I knew too much as a first responder chaplain not to be alarmed. There are 1,500 child kidnappings each year. About 250 of them are classified as a "stranger abduction", also known as a "non-family abduction", which is the result of a stranger taking or luring a child.

45

90% of children abducted by strangers make it home safe and sound. But at that moment in the parking lot, I could only think of those 10% of the cases where the children do not.

My panic button had most definitely been pushed, as I convinced myself that Trevor was in that van. I yelled for Heidi as I was contemplating some sort of Tom Cruise impromptu move to chase down the van. Unfortunately, there were no motorcycles or helicopters anywhere in sight. Right then I heard Heidi call from the parking lot where our van was located (our non-creepy Chevy Astro van), "We found him!!" The little bugger had walked out of the store and was huddled on the other side of our van out of our sight the whole time. Phew!

Lying in bed, my mind drifted back to little Annie, and Don and Joan. And God.

I taught people in church that God is good and all-powerful. We would sing songs titled "God is Good All the Time" and lyrics that proclaimed, "God will make a way where there seems to be no way." But what about the missing children who are never rescued or found dead. Is God "good" then? Why didn't God "make a way" for those innocent children? Will the parents of these children think of God as good and all-powerful? Should they? Would I have, if the circumstances with Trevor had turned out tragically different?

Every scene I show up at as a first responder defies the tidy theological explanations I once confidently preached to others as a church pastor.

There is a rather obscure book and story in the Old Testament of the Bible, the Book of Ruth. The story is about a woman named Naomi who is forced by famine to move her family from their homeland and seek refuge in a nearby but unknown country. Suddenly and tragically, the woman's husband dies and a few years later her two children also die, leaving Naomi alone, destitute, and fearful in a foreign land. Ruth, who is Naomi's now-widowed daughter-in-law, vows to look after and care for Naomi. The biblical writer of the story uses the Hebrew word 'hesed' (lovingkindness) to describe Ruth's commitment to Naomi, which is a term typically used to describe God.

Speaking of God, he is conspicuously absent in the story. The bottom falls out of Naomi's life and God is nowhere to be found. The biblical writer does not offer any explanation of this random and harrowing tragedy with respect to God. Nothing! This story never really made any sense to me and I cannot remember ever giving a sermon about it. But then one day it hit me. God was not absent in the story. God was Ruth. The love, mercy, goodness, strength, kindness, and loyalty of God showed up in, as, and through Ruth. I realized God never promised that our human journey would be absent of suffering. God never guaranteed that at all times that journey would even make sense. God never stipulated that there would always be a sufficient explanation.

God only promised to show up.

It was useless trying to sleep at home, with Annie on my mind. I decided to call over to one of the police officers I knew over at Don's house to see if there were any new updates. Regrettably, there were not. Day two was over. No Annie.

DAY THREE

As I greeted Don and Joan the next morning, I noted the desperate and exhausted look upon their faces. It was now the third day that Annie had gone missing, and there was no sign or clue of her whereabouts. The grim possibility of foul play and her death was bearing down upon them with each passing hour. Television news stations continued following the story and showed Annie's picture on every newscast.

The situations that police officers, firefighters, paramedics, and SAR (Search and Rescue) teams are faced with are inherently difficult, stressful, and traumatic. Many situations involve gruesome scenes of death. These individuals often provide emotional as well as physical support to traumatized survivors. Although they have received specialized training for this kind of work, beneath their uniform, badge, and gear, they are human beings and are affected by these tragic incidents. PTSD, anxiety, depression, substance abuse, and divorce are the mental health collateral damage that occurs. First responders, including police officers and firefighters, are more likely to die by suicide than in the line of duty.

Missing children cases are often the most traumatizing. You get attached to the people involved. As a parent yourself, as many first responders are, you suffer right alongside them. You are vested in the desired outcome, hoping against all hope that the child will be returned home.

My work as a chaplain is a deep commitment to supporting these brave men and women who sacrifice themselves to save others, and aid those in need and crisis. As a former firefighter myself, I understand the emotional toll it takes. There are many barriers that often prevent first responders from receiving the mental health support they need. Denial, stigma on the job, fear of job loss, financial concerns, and access to treatment are some of the obstacles. I view my role as the first line of defense. As a first responder chaplain I try to build a good rapport with these men and women and let them know I am available to talk if they are struggling. One of the most important contributions I can make is to help them take the necessary steps to receive proper mental health support and services.

Everyone was keeping an optimistic spirit about Annie. And then mid-afternoon, word came in that Annie had been sighted. Security cameras had caught her image arriving at a BART subway station in

San Francisco, 25 miles from Danville. Cameras also captured her getting on a train car with her bicycle, headed into the city.

This information raised more questions than it answered. Should it be taken as good news or grim news? It appeared Annie was alone. Why would she travel to San Francisco by herself without telling anyone?

There was a shift of focus in the investigation, and suddenly Don and Joan were being asked about the recent mental state of Annie. Had she had a conflict at home or school? Did she seem down or depressed lately? Had she ever spoken about being bullied? Is there a reason she would have run away from home? Each question got more agonizing to answer. It had to be considered. Could it be possible that she was headed to the Golden Gate Bridge?

The Golden Gate Bridge is the second-most used suicide site in the world. Since the bridge's opening in 1937, there have been more than 1,700 confirmed suicides and 300 unconfirmed. The fatality rate of jumping is over 98%. A number of measures are in place to discourage people from jumping, including telephone hotlines and patrols by emergency personnel and bridge workers. On average, the Bridge Patrol or the California Highway Patrol stops someone from jumping every two or three days.

A few hours later, Don and Joan received the devastating and heartbreaking news; Annie's bicycle was found parked and locked to a bike rack at the Golden Gate Bridge. A homeland security camera located under the bridge captured the image of her falling from the bridge.

Annie's death was classified as a suicide. Her body was never found. Gone, without a trace.

DAY 12

A parent never fully "recovers" from the traumatic death of their child, especially a suicide. Shock, denial, guilt, regret, anger, and depression are a normal part of their grief. "Oh God, the sea is so great and my boat is so small."

I have learned a few lessons about the grieving process. There is no timeline. Every person's grieving process is unique to them; it cannot be planned, forced, condensed, or bypassed. There is no "life hack" for grief. Shakespeare wrote, "To weep is to make less the depth of grief." As a chaplain, I am often simply creating a space for another human to feel what they feel, to inhabit their heartache and suffering, and release it in the presence of another human being who cares.

I learned another lesson. There is no answer. The twelfth day after the news of Annie's death, I was having coffee with Don. I wanted to check in with him to see how he and Joan were doing. And that is when he asked me the question, "Why did God let this happen?"

Annie's death left many questions for which there will never be a sufficient answer. Perhaps Don's specific question about God was the most troubling. Was God being "good" and "all-powerful" when Annie plunged to her death? What could the suicide of a 15-year-old girl possibly accomplish in the infinite wisdom and plan of God?

I was uncertain about what Don did or did not believe about God. I inquired into his religious background, to which he responded, "I used to go to church." He shared he had grown up Catholic, attended parochial schools, but found little use for religion when he came of age. Despite having no active involvement in organized religion, his most pressing question about Annie's death was related to God, "Why did God let this happen?"

Like Naomi's tragedy, God seemed cruelly absent and silent. What frustrated me about that biblical story was the same frustration with Annie's death. God was nowhere to be found. At the very moment of desperation, he was needed most, the situation you would think a merciful and caring God would most act, it was like he vanished without a trace. No divine intervention. No miracle. No explanation. Nothing.

I could not give Don an answer. Years ago, as a pastor, I had an answer for everything. I sometimes wonder if this is the reason so many people leave church. Everyone dresses up, puts on a happy smile, speak Christianese, act like they have it together, and pretend to know all the answers. I think people eventually see through this make-believe world. It does not square with the realities of life in the real world, lacks credibility and of little use.

Maybe the evidence that God is real, good, and all-powerful is not that God spares us from tragedy, heartache and suffering. Maybe it's that he shows up in it. And maybe not through miraculous intervention but the lovingkindness and solidarity we give to one another. Maybe you and I are God to one another… in the real world. I believe that.

We sat. We wept. We mourned. We embraced. We parted.

Later that night at home, Heidi asked how Don and Joan were doing. I shared a little about my visit with Don. Heidi mentioned that she had read something earlier in the day that said the name 'Annie' means grace.

That is the number one requirement of a first responder chaplain— the grace to admit that you do not have all the answers and the grace to show up in the absence of them.

CHAPTER 3

I DIDN'T SIGN
UP FOR THIS

Martin Luther wrote, "Every man must do two things alone; he must do his own believing and his own dying."

He is right, and he is not. Of course, it is true that every human being's death is an individual, lone, and unshared occurrence. No one can die for you. No one dies with you. There will come a moment when the biological functions that sustain you as a living being will cease. Only you will experience that moment for yourself. That does not mean every person dies unaccompanied when that time comes. If you are fortunate, perhaps your last moments on earth are spent surrounded by those you love.

Typically, a person cannot choose when or how they die. Mark did not expect to die on the side of the road that fateful May evening. Nor did he expect to die in the arms of a stranger. But he did. And that stranger was me.

The fire dispatch call came out on my Motorola two-way radio as a "Priority 2" incident. Priority 3 is walking wounded; Priority 2 is moderate to serious injury or illness, but not life-threatening; Priority

1 is life-threatening. I have had more Priority 1 scenarios than I care to remember. I will take a Priority 2 or 3 any day.

It was a Saturday night when my brother, Leo, and wife, Perla, were visiting us in Austin. Being a volunteer firefighter and EMT for our local fire department meant we were permitted to respond to calls in our own personal vehicles. I was given a siren and red light to pop on my car roof whenever I was dispatched to a medical or fire emergency. On this particular night we were all together watching a movie at our home when my fire department radio blasted an alarm for a Code 3, Priority 2 incident, involving a cyclist. Code 3 means use lights and siren, and as mentioned, Priority 2 indicates non-life-threatening injury.

Austin, home to Lance Armstrong, is known as a cycling city. Even with the numerous bike lanes, occasionally there is a cycling incident when someone is injured. Thankfully, the one I was called to respond to was not serious. Since it was not a life-threatening situation, I thought it would be cool to have Leo and Perla come along. Afterall, who gets to take their family on a Code 3 drive with lights and sirens? It was likely a common injury associated with a fall. No big deal.

Speeding down Bee Cave Road, lights flashing and siren screaming, the sun had set, and darkness had settled in. A quarter mile from the incident, I could see there were multiple emergency vehicles. Not what I expected for a Priority 2.

As we came to a stop near the scene, a firefighter was tending to a young man lying in the middle of the roadway. I cautioned my family to stay in the car until I checked things out. Grabbing my medic bag, I ran to join the firefighter tending to this distressed and agitated cyclist, his mangled bike next to him. Typically, you try not to move a victim until paramedics arrive.

I also noticed on the side of the road an old 70's Chevy El Camino truck, which was missing one of its side decorative metal bars. It was obviously the vehicle involved in the collision. As we began to assess the victim, I heard the distinct sound of chopper blades in the distance. Sheriff's deputies were in the streets stopping traffic; Austin's Life Flight helicopter had been called in. An additional firetruck and paramedic ambulance came flashing and howling.

This was no Priority 2!

The subject was a 24-year-old male named Mark. He had been riding down Bee Cave Road when the El Camino drifted into the bike lane and struck him. He was lying face down in his cycling gear, groaning. I suspected he broke his collarbone, an excruciating injury. The firefighter and I decided to gently roll the young man over to further assess his condition. As we turned him, a metal bar protruding from his torso became visible, which the firefighter had not noticed until then.

The driver sideswiped the cyclist and he was instantly impaled with the decorative spear-like bar, which had detached from the side of the low-profile truck. He had been knocked to the ground with a metal bar extruding from his chest, fighting for his life.

Two paramedics hustled over from their ambulance and instructed me to hold the young man still while they inserted an IV into his arm. Now pitch dark outside, the deafening helicopter hovered above this perilous scene with its floodlights beaming down upon us. Sirens, lights, shouting, chaos, trauma; what started as a fairly routine call had turned into a MASH unit. This is not what I meant for my family to witness. I was so absorbed in this triage at hand that I had forgotten they were even there.

A good friend of mine, Kevin, who followed in my footsteps as a volunteer firefighter and only a few weeks on the job, arrived on the scene and was asked to hold the IV bag while myself and the paramedics tried to stabilize the young man. Suddenly, the young man was seized by hysteria, screaming, and choking, "I can't breathe!"

Oxygen was being ripped from his lungs. Mark had gone into respiratory arrest, which possibly meant he was also in cardiac arrest. With the metal bar speared in his chest, he was drowning from internal bleeding.

The Life Flight helicopter landed a few yards away. The young man was stretched across my lap, fighting, and gasping for every breath. I exhorted him, "Stay with us, Mark! Hang in there! We're going to get you out of here!" He was quickly losing the battle. We began CPR, and heard the orders, "Hot load! Hot load!," which meant we were going to attempt to load Mark on the helicopter while it was still running and rotors spinning. "Don't die on me, Mark! Hang in there! We're gonna take a ride!"

But Mark could hold on no longer. There was no more fight left in him. We did everything we could, but it was too little and too late. Lights flashing, sirens screaming, chopper blades thrumming, voices shouting, Mark died in my arms in the middle of the road on that Saturday night in May. Face to face, as he laid in my lap, I watched him relinquish his life. Breath by labored breath, I escorted Mark to his end.

I have been asked several times what it's like to watch someone die. In traumatic cases of a violent death such as this, it is vexing. Cradling and watching Mark's last gasps for life is a scene that has been seared in my memory. I will never be able to expunge his voice and words from my consciousness, "I can't breathe!"

Lying in the street, with this young man's lifeless body in my arms, I felt an icy numbness coursing through my veins. I was gutted, and shut my eyes in physical, mental, and emotional exhaustion. Everything stopped. The world fell deafeningly quiet, and empty, and heavy, and cruel. Somewhere in the distance there was a world happening, while I was free-falling into an abyss of anguish.

154,000 people in our world die every day. That is 110 people every minute. We all know that every human being born into the world, dies. None of us are unclear about this fundamental fact of human existence. But when someone we love dies; we feel utterly unprepared for it. It happens to everyone, and yet when death rips from our lives a person we love, we feel robbed, assailed, and forsaken. We look for someone or something to blame. But who? Robbed by life? Forsaken by God? Swindled by the universe? As a chaplain for many years I have at times blamed myself. Maybe if I had gotten to Mark five minutes sooner, maybe if I had done more, maybe if I had taken a different measure, maybe if I could have better stabilized his hysteria, maybe if..."

I knew virtually nothing about Mark. Was this lifeless body in my lap someone's father, someone's son, someone's husband, someone's brother? We grieve deeply when we lose a person who matters to us but holding Mark in those moments it hit me that every human being matters. Each of those 154,000 human beings who died today, matter.

As a chaplain, I do not traffic in "answers." Instead, I have learned to make peace with the world as it is and have faith that it means more than the way it appears and feels in any given moment. There is a lot I do not and never will understand about life, existence, and the human journey, but there are a few things I know that are true of every person alive, including you the reader. You matter. You have a life. You will die. You do not know when. These facts are reason enough to hold your life and every life, reverently, compassionately, and spartanly. Greek philosopher Seneca wrote, "Begin at once to live, and count each separate day as a separate life." Maybe the gift that comes with death, is we learn to love life more.

"Nick! Nick, you okay?," I felt a hand on my shoulder. The paramedic jolted me back to reality—sweat, blood, lights, sirens, police radios, chopper blades, shouting. They removed Mark from my lap, lifted him onto a gurney, and carted him away. Then he was gone. Gone from the scene. Gone from the earth. Gone!

In the chaos, I looked up at my friend Kevin, a newbie firefighter, who was standing above me in his firefighter bunker gear. Kevin had turned his life around after spending seven years in one of the most violent prisons in Texas. He was tough as nails. But I will never forget the chilling look on his face and what he said, "I didn't sign up for this!"

Kevin's words had particular meaning to our work as first responders. No one chooses to be a first responder because we want to witness or be a part of someone else's tragedy or death. We do this because we want to rescue, save, and protect people, and come to their aid in moments of dire need. It is not in our mind to tend to a person for whom death is certain, but to exhaust every possibility to prevent their death. We did everything we could to save Mark, but rather than avert his death, we watched him die. Kevin's words were true, we didn't sign up for this.

But there was something deeper in his words that each of us can identify with. It speaks to the reality of the human situation. When we experience a tragic loss or have our hearts broken, when we are struck down by hardship or catastrophe, when we suffer rejection or betrayal, when our lives are reduced to a pile of rubble or our dreams dashed to the ground, when the world feels cruel, heartless and indifferent, in times of darkness, hopelessness or despair, a voice cries out from deep within us, "I didn't sign up for this!" Life can be beautiful, rapturous, blissful, and transcendent. But there are also I-didn't-sign-up-for-this moments. For every chaplain call I respond to, there is someone having one of those moments.

The truth is, I *did* sign up for this. I knew full well that being a first responder chaplain meant tragedy, trauma, and death. The whole point of being a chaplain is coming alongside people with comfort, compassion, and support in those very moments. It does not mean I like the fact that people are stricken by loss, heartache, and suffering, but I signed up to stand with them in those times.

I see the worst of human suffering on a regular basis. I have no illusions about how fragile, precarious, and perilous the human predicament can be. Yet every morning, I get up ready to do it all over again. One day I realized that I *did* sign-up for this, I enlisted in another day of life, another day of being human, another day in a world that is both beautiful and tragic. A lot of it I do not like and most of it I cannot explain, but I am choosing it. I am a card-carrying member of a long line of the human species, who have been signing up for this since the beginning of time.

It occurred to me one day that the choice to sign up is to choose God. That maybe God is the primal will to live. Today 154,000 people will die: it could be me, could be you, could be your child, spouse, parent, or best friend. Yet, each of us starts over again every day, in spite of all we know, against all we know. Why?

E.E. Cummings wrote, "Unbeing dead isn't being alive." What is the "being alive" part that is distinctly more than simply being "undead"? There is something within us that is more than the activity of our lungs in breathing and the functioning of our arteries to pump blood. There is a part of us that wills to love, have compassion, act courageously, experience beauty, be kindhearted, find meaning, live nobly, become ourselves fully, know belonging, taste transcendence. What is *that* part—the part that signs up for life where a young man pedals out of his driveway on a carefree May evening, never to make it back home again?

There came a point in my life when I stopped being disappointed with God about all the world's terrible tragedies and hardships, including those in my own life, that made no sense and defied any reasonable explanation. Instead, I started finding God in my desire to walk into that world each day and be fully alive with love, compassion, and courage. My life changed when I realized that God was not making me do this, but I wanted to myself. I want to be alive. Not just undead but truly and fully alive.

The helicopter was lifting off, and Kevin helped me to my feet. We were both spent. Amidst the lights and sirens, I reached out to give him a hug. There is a unique and unbreakable bond you feel with those who choose to do this work. As we stood there, I spotted Heidi and the family down the street. In all the chaos, I had completely forgotten they were there. Sweat and blood on my face, Heidi's eyes welled up in tears as I walked toward her. I came undone, standing there in the middle of Bee Cave Road.

I do not know what will kill me first—the beauty of this world or the sorrow of it. There is a bliss that no amount of ache can steal away. And there is an ache that no amount of bliss can rescue you from. The deal is both the beauty, and the sorrow. It is what it means to be fully alive. You are supposed to feel both the bliss and the ache. Life is not supposed to make sense; it is supposed to make you more fully human.

A person could ask why God allows suffering in our world. But we could also ask why we would choose to keep living in it. People often think of God with the former question, and never give any thought to God with the latter one.

Martin Luther did not quite cover all the bases. Yes, there are the two things he said we do alone—we do our own believing and we do our own dying. There is a third. We do our own living.

That is what we signed up for.

CHAPTER 4

B-E-L-I-E-V-E

Human beings believe things.

We have beliefs about weighty matters like the meaning of life and what is beyond the grave. We have beliefs about lesser issues like who makes the best pizza, or which smartphone is superior, iPhone or Android. We do not give a second thought to some of our beliefs. The sun rising tomorrow is never in question, we just believe it will rise.

A belief is an acceptance that something exists or is true. Belief normally implies the absence of doubt. I believe I will one day die. I am certain of it. At some point in time there will be a termination of all my biological functions that sustain me as a living organism. I have plenty of evidence to substantiate my belief.

There may not be factual certainty that something is true, but that does not stop a person from believing it. Contrary to popular belief, if you are hit by a penny dropped from the Empire State Building it will not kill you. Lightning does strike the same place twice and many more times than that. Despite the National Enquirer, there is no proof that Elvis is still alive, notwithstanding the recent citing at a Dairy Queen outside Memphis. And of course, there is the five-second rule—if you drop food on the floor and pick it up within five seconds it is safe to eat. However, research shows that salmonella can survive on the floor for weeks. I suggest you follow the no-second rule.

Our beliefs shape and determine our experience of life and the world. Johann Wolfgang von Goethe wrote, "A man sees in the world what he carries in his heart." If you believe something is true, whether it really is or not, it is true for you. For centuries people believed the world was flat and feared the possibility of falling off the edge of the earth into an abyss of nothingness. A person is governed, and often limited by the beliefs he or she chooses.

One of the most prevailing beliefs a person has is their belief about God. What one believes about God can determine what a person thinks about themselves, the purpose and meaning of life, and what happens when you die. A belief about God can engender fear, shame, and bigotry, or inspire love, peace, beauty, and compassion.

Did it ever occur to you that you can choose your beliefs about God? Chances are that you did not choose the beliefs about God you have right now, but learned or inherited them from your family, culture, or religious background. Setting aside different beliefs about God across the spectrum of the world's religions, within Christianity itself there are thousands of denominations worldwide that believe different things about God.

What do you believe about God? What factors influenced your beliefs? Are your beliefs about God consciously and deliberately chosen, or did you inherit them from others?

These questions hit me in a way they never had before when I noticed atop a fireplace mantle—in separate big brass letters—the spelled-out word "B-E-L-I-E-V-E."

Living in Austin, one early morning a couple of weeks before Christmas, while having breakfast with friends, my pager buzzed. It read: "Priority 1 Cardiac Arrest. Chaplain needed. 331 Sycamore Avenue." Taking a few final gulps of coffee, I excused myself and promptly headed to the address.

A cardiac arrest rarely ends with a "save." When the chaplain is dispatched, it usually means a death has occurred, and they need me to console the family. As much as I see my chaplaincy work as a calling for moments just like this, a part of me would rather be anywhere else on the planet besides a place of death and grief.

Chaplain calls are full of emotion for everyone involved. The focus is on those at the scene who are fresh in anguish and despair. Meanwhile, the chaplain must keep a check on his or her own emotions, which is not always easy to do given the disturbing situations we often encounter. Even with all our training and experience, chaplains are still human beings, and it is impossible to check our emotions at the door. I assumed this call involved an adult, most likely an older male which is a common cardiac arrest scenario in the early mornings.

My assumption was wrong.

Typically, when called by dispatch, I ask, "What is the age? Male or female? Nature of the death? Who is at the residence?" Those are the most pertinent questions for me. But in this case, I did not ask.

I cannot ever remember a scene as eerie as this one. Pulling up to the house, there was a sea of flashing lights from police and sheriff cars, firetruck, and ambulance. But despite all these emergency vehicles, you could hear a pin drop. Outside the house there was a haunting hush and an unsettling stillness.

The fire chief came out the front door, and as he approached me, I asked, "What do we have?" A grim expression filled his face, and he said in a low and somber tone, "This is a bad one, Nick. The Osborne family. A 10-year-old boy died suddenly from an unknown cause. His mother and father, along with two younger sisters, are inside the home. It's not good."

My heart sank. The death of a child is always the most intense and disturbing. I braced myself as I stepped through the open front door. How people display severe grief varies. You never know what to expect. The scene of every tragedy feels like holy ground. The personal space where a person is cracked open by catastrophic loss is one in which you tread lightly, respectfully, and humbly.

The first thing that caught my eye was the sight of a mother draped over the body of her son laying in the middle of the living room floor. As a first responder chaplain of twenty-one years, there is a part of every tragic scene that becomes a part of me, usually in the form of images like this. At the most inopportune times—sitting at a stop light, at a dinner party, the middle of the night—these snapshots will intrude upon my mind.

The house was full of police officers, sheriff's deputies, firefighters, and paramedics, all standing around the perimeter of the room and into the kitchen with looks of unbelief written on their faces. They had tried their best to revive the young boy but to no avail. Grief and despair were the outcomes through no fault of their own, but that does not mitigate some measure of remorse they feel for failing to resuscitate the young boy.

Everyone looks in my direction as the paramedic steps over to brief me on who is who and what happened. I can see the relief in the eyes of the first responders that someone "official" had arrived to deal with the distraught parents.

I stood motionless, uncertain how to begin a dialogue with a mother who is hemorrhaging with heartache and undone with grief, laying over her son. Who am I to even consider interrupting this? Searching the room for the father, someone points out that he is down the hall making phone calls. For the moment he is preoccupied with the task of communicating with relatives, but I can hear his anguish as he explains this nightmare to loved ones. The agony in his voice pierces the whole house.

Over the years, I have learned to fight the urge to interject myself into a situation, and patiently wait for an opportunity to be meaningfully present. As a chaplain. you must be attentive to what is occurring in the moment. I was not sensing it was time to interrupt the grieving mother and continued scouting the room, noticing the pictures hanging on the walls and the Christmas decorations.

After a few minutes, the mother turned her head in the direction where I was standing, and we made eye contact. I moved closer to introduce myself, reverently bending down on one knee beside her on the floor. For the first time, the boy came into my full view. I studied his face, his features, his pale soft skin, his wavy blonde hair. For a moment I saw my son, Trenton, in the boy's face. They looked to be about the same age, and the resemblance was chilling. There are moments when it hits you that the same tragedies that strike others every day could just as likely be yours.

I reached out and gently placed my hand on the mother's shoulder and introduced myself, "Mrs. Osborne, my name is Nick, and I am the chaplain for our police and fire department. I am sorry about your son." She could hardly respond as she looked up with swollen, tear-filled eyes, grimacing with anguish. I have seen this look far too many times that I care to remember.

There is no script for a first responder chaplain. You go with your intuition. At that moment I feel an openness to lay down on the floor next to her son. She says, "I don't know what to do? What do I do?" Letting her question sink in, I respond, "Right now you are doing what you need to do. Just be here on the floor close to your son." She protests, "How can I go on? I can't do this. My sweet Ian. Why? This can't be real."

Gently stroking my hand through her son's blonde hair, I said, "Ian is such a handsome boy." I slowly reclined on my side next to him, while she laid on his other side. With his body between us, I could see both his face and hers, as she kissed his forehead and tears of heartbreak dropped from her cheeks onto his. I eventually broke the silence by asking her a few questions about her son, their family, and the two younger girls.

Laying on the floor as we talked, I noticed on the fireplace mantle—in separate big brass letters—the spelled-out word "B-E-L-I-E-V-E." It is such a common word; a simple verb, which means to accept or have confidence in something as true. The word felt discomforting as it towered above the scene on the floor. "Believe what?" I thought to myself. Was this a religious family who believed in God? Was it a Christmastime sentiment for the children; the anticipation of Santa's goodies on Christmas morning? And what was the relevance of this word for a mother grieving the death of her son?

After a while consoling mom, I got up and searched for the father. Tending to his two younger daughters in their back bedroom was serving as a temporary distraction from the acute pangs of emotional pain. I poked my head in the door and introduced myself to him. After some friendly banter with the girls, he and I stepped out to talk.

People have different reactions when I introduce myself as a chaplain; they are mostly appreciative, knowing I intend to offer comfort and emotional support. Likely, they will also think of me as a member of the clergy, which could either be positive or negative, depending upon their religious background and experience.

One way I have found to build trust with a person in a traumatic situation is to offer my support in practical ways. I asked the father if there was something specific I could help them with right away. He needed help sorting out what would happen next. The mother overheard our conversation and came over. I delicately explained that the medical examiner would arrive within the hour to take the boy's body downtown for examination. Following this, the body would be released to a funeral home.

There is typically great distress for the family when the medical examiner arrives. The separation of the body from the home is an unforgiving moment for the family and often an unbearable scene to watch. I did my best to prepare them to say their goodbyes, knowing that the removal of the body will reignite the volatility of their loss and heartache. Everyone on the scene was on edge, bracing themselves for what was coming. When the medical examiner arrives, the first responders will typically leave. Everyone, except me.

When the medical examiner pulled up to the house, I encouraged the parents to spend a final few moments with their deceased son, and then tend to their two younger girls. It is torturous for a parent to watch their child zipped up in a body bag and taken away. I do my best to prevent this situation but do not always succeed. Even for a seasoned chaplain like myself, it is a traumatic ordeal. By the time the medical examiner was finished, friends and extended family members had arrived to offer their emotional support. The mother and father did not see the examination and the removal of the boy's body, but when they re-entered the room and their son was no longer there, the floodgates of grief burst wide open.

With their friends and family members present, it was time for me to consider how to depart the scene. You never leave a situation feeling like your work is done or that things are "okay" enough for you to go. Losing a child is not "okay." It will not be "okay" tomorrow or the day after that. It will not be "okay" next week or next month. It will not be "okay," ever.

I had a conversation with the Osborne's to say my goodbyes. Giving them my card, I assured them that they could call me at any time. I promised to follow-up with them, which I did over the next several days and weeks. You cannot help but become personally invested in these tragedies. Having been there several hours, I began to build a meaningful connection with both mom and dad. There is an intimate bond that is forged in the crucible of suffering. I felt particularly attached to this traumatic event, being a father myself of a son the same age as Ian.

The theology I learned in seminary and preached in church often falls short in the tragedies I encounter as a first responder chaplain. A safe distance removed from the suffering of the world, I sliced and diced the hardships of life into the theological categories of God's "perfect will," and God's "permissive will." God's "perfect will" is God's perfect plan for each of us and the entire created order. It is a reality of goodness, harmony, peace, and joy, and the absence of all evil and suffering. The Bible depicts or represents this state of being in descriptions such as the Garden of Eden and Heaven. There is also God's "permissive will," which is what God is willing to allow in the short-term before this perfect scenario emerges. God's "permissive will" means that an all-powerful God chooses not to prevent or intervene amidst life's hardships and suffering.

Suppose I had tried to explain this concept to the Osborne's as some sort of defense of God and faith, in light of the death of their son. Most parents will not have to bury their children, so why was Ian's death on God's "permissive will" list? Let me ask you, if you could have prevented Ian's death, would you have? Or would you have allowed it? Would you be okay with God "permitting" the loss of your child?

While we are at it, we would have to add to God's permissible list, every horrific, heartbreaking, traumatic incident I have ever been called to as a first responder chaplain. Further still, consider what other horrors are on God's "permissive will" list: Holocaust; 9/11; Rwandan genocide; human trafficking; starvation; war; slavery; child abuse; teen suicide, to name but a few. Would a God of love, goodness, mercy, protection, and justice, sign-off on the Holocaust an okay thing to happen?

See the problem here?

Those block letters displayed across the mantle in the Osborne home, confront me: B-E-L-I-E-V-E.

Believe what?

What is a heartbroken mother swathed over the body of her dead ten-year-old son supposed to believe? Should she have faith in a God who saw fit to have the death of her son on his permissible list? Should she be afraid for what else she loves that made it on the list? There is a Bible verse that states that God will not give you more than you are capable of enduring. Seriously? Is it necessary for God to test the theory to this degree? Is that what a merciful and loving God would do?

When I got back to the house, Heidi was on the phone discussing plans with her sister who was coming to celebrate the Christmas holiday at our home. I poured myself a cup of coffee and sat down at the kitchen table to return a few emails. One of my firefighter friends had emailed me about getting a group of guys together to attend an Oakland Raiders game. As I was scouting out their home game dates, I peered over the top of my laptop screen and my eyes caught a wood pallet sign Heidi had hung on the front room wall for Christmas. The sign had the word "Immanuel" stenciled across it.

For a few moments I pondered this word. It is used in the Bible in association with the birth of Jesus. The twenty-third verse in the first chapter of Matthew's Gospel reads, "The virgin will be with child and will give birth to a son, and they will call him Immanuel—which means, 'God with us.'" God with us.

Too often, the traditional view of God comes off feeling like God is a superhuman being somewhere over the rainbow and off yonder in the neverlands, managing the cosmic affairs of the universe. Two common beliefs about God that I view as false and detrimental, is that God is somewhere up in the sky and we are separate from him. God was pleased to accept the term "Immanuel" for a name to reveal the truth that God is with us where we are, and there is no separation.

I have studied the Bible that my Christianity is based upon, and I cannot find any place where God says that our human journey will be or should be absent of hardship, adversity, tragedy, loss, and suffering. To the contrary, God tells us that our lifetime on earth will include difficulty. The hardship, difficulty and suffering that Jesus himself experienced is evidence of this fact. Saint Paul, who authored the bulk of the New Testament, endured many severe trials and tribulations.

Rather than some cosmic deity up in the sky somewhere, dispassionately seeing human suffering as a function of his permissive will, God joins the human journey in the flesh as Jesus and he is not spared this same suffering. Too often, Christianity makes the story of God about how he is going to save us from the world but overlooks the story of how he joins us in it. "Immanuel" does not mean "God distant from us," "God separated from us," "God looking down upon us" or "God insulating us." No, Immanuel means, "God WITH us."

Jesus often proclaimed, "The kingdom of God has come." People looked around, taking note of all the hardships of the world and their own difficulties, and said they could see no such kingdom. To which Jesus responded, they were looking in the wrong place. He told them they had to look within themselves to find the kingdom of God. Jesus said, you find the love, goodness, grace, compassion, strength, and peace of God inside yourself. In other words, God is not only "with" us, God is "within" us.

Did you realize that any God you find inside a church you brought in yourself? Likewise, I know that God is present at every scene before I ever arrive. And I know that I am an expression of the life of God within me through my work as first responder chaplain.

Charles Dickens' novella, *A Christmas Carol*, is a classic Christmas story. But I am also reminded of his other well-known book, *A Tale of Two Cities*, which opens with these words, "It was the best of times, it was the worst of times…" That about sums up the human journey, don't you think?

Ian was a gift to the Osborne family for ten years—it was the best of times. His life was tragically cut short—it was the worst of times. The joy of his life does not spare them the heartache of his death. But their tragic loss will never diminish the happiness of the time they had together. God was there for all of it, both the joy and the grief.

A couple of days following Ian's death, I received a phone call one evening from Mr. Osborne. He apologized for ringing late, but I assured him he could contact me at any time, day, or night. He explained he had a request to make of me. He asked me to officiate Ian's memorial service the following week. I was deeply touched by his petition and accepted.

Over a thousand classmates and community friends attended Ian's memorial service. It was one of the most heartrending and beautiful occasions I have ever experienced. I was moved by what this young boy meant to so many people in the short life he had lived.

In my remarks at the service, I shared about the word B-E-L-I-E-V-E, spelled out across the mantle in the Osborne home. Each of us experiences suffering, hardship, and loss in life. It may not be the death of a child; it could be the end of a marriage, a serious health issue, financial misfortune, depression, addiction, injustice, loneliness, rejection, or the loss of a loved one. In moments like these, what do we believe about ourselves, about life, about God?

What if we believed that God is not watching us from somewhere in the sky above, but he is with us in every moment. Rather than believing that God could never understand our pain and suffering, what if we believed he endured it all himself. What if we stopped thinking that we find God within the four walls of a church, but we find him inside ourselves.

I am not trying to tell you what to believe about God. I am asking you to consider the possibility that to "believe" may not be the assurance that God will spare you of suffering but knowing that God walks with you through it. To "believe" may not mean expecting divine intervention from on high when we struggle, but expressing that kingdom of compassion, empathy, solidarity, and tenderness within ourselves, to one another in moments of grief, heartache, and suffering.

The most important questions about God are not answered in creeds or sorted out in elaborate theological constructions. People are often searching for answers outside themselves, but maybe the answers we most want, and need are within us. Those answers may not be clear all at once, and we have to live ourselves into them. Maybe this is what it means to B-E-L-I-E-V-E.

CHAPTER 5

THROWN INTO THE FIRE

Religion at its worst induces the fear of God. The Book of Revelation conjures up images of sinners being "thrown into the lake of fire." Hellfire preaching uses the fear of eternal torture in the flames of Hell to manipulate non-believers to convert to Christianity. I was once a church pastor myself. Rather than being the hellfire preacher, I was the one thrown into the fire… literally.

On one of my first Sundays as a pastor in Austin, Texas I preached a sermon which included a story of fighting a fierce structure fire when I was a young man serving as a reserve firefighter. Several men in the congregation who were volunteer firefighters for the local fire district approached me after the sermon with an invitation to attend a meeting hoping I would consider becoming a volunteer again. I resisted for six months after their repeated attempts to lure me to a meeting. I finally gave in and agreed to go just to "check it out."

After the meeting, the fire chief put on a full-court press to coax me into joining the department. He presented me with a whole set of brand-new firefighting gear—boots, pants, jacket, helmet, gloves, as well as a pager and radio. It worked.

My next hairbrained idea was stealthily putting on all my fire-fighter gear in the garage when I got home that evening and bursting through the back-door yelling, "Firefighter dad is home! I've come to rescue you!" My children were toddlers and you should have seen the look on their faces. I scooped them both up, one in each arm, as if I was rescuing them yelling, "I'll save you!!" It was hilarious!

Heidi was not amused.

With a dumbfounded look written across her face, she said, "Really, Nick?" She reminded me that I was over 40, had a bad back, and calmly suggested that perhaps it was time to grow up. Later that night she asked, "So, what do you do if the radio goes off and there is a call?" Hmmm. Good question. I had not thought it through that far yet. I answered, "I don't know. They didn't say."

The very next night just after dark we were standing in the kitchen and the fire radio sounded an alert. A voice came over the radio, "CE-Bar Fire and Rescue, respond to a structure fire!" Heidi looked at me and asked, "What are you going to do?" I thought about it for a second and said, "I'm now a firefighter! I'm going!"

I jumped into my Ford Taurus and headed to the location. I was not sure what I was going to do when I got there. I had not quite thought it through that far yet.

The ominous glow of a large residential structure fire lit up the nighttime sky a mile away from the scene. As I came within a few blocks of the raging inferno I found a place to park in the neighborhood and suited up in my new firefighter gear. Residents crowded the street watching the fire, as I trotted through them toward the blaze.

There are around 1,216,600 firefighters serving in 27,228 fire departments nationwide and responding to emergencies from 58,150 fire stations. Of those firefighters, 31% are career firefighters and 69% are volunteers. A Fire department responds to a fire every 23 seconds throughout the United States. Firefighters experience a steady onslaught of trauma and intense human emotion. Perilous flames, collapsing buildings, the anguish of burn victims, explosions, automobile accidents, suicide attempts, and even terrorist attacks. Such harrowing events come with the territory of first responders. On average, firefighters will work 10, 24-hour shifts per month. Firefighters do not get holidays off.

There are six known classes of fires. Some include gases, liquids, metals, and oils. Each one requires a different approach and it is up to the firefighters to decipher which type of fire they are dealing with. After subduing the flames, firefighters are tasked with finding the cause. They discover the starting point of a fire by using their knowledge of fire and deductive skills. They use their scientific knowledge of chemistry, physics, and engineering to deduce where and when a fire started. Besides pinpointing the origin, firefighters can also determine if a fire occurred by accident or arson.

First responders risk their lives daily to serve the public. Many times, their risks and sacrifices go unnoticed and unappreciated. A firefighter never knows for sure if he or she will return to their family at the end of a shift. In a moment, a firefighter's life may be in grave danger, but they endure this for us. Usually an unsung hero, a firefighter may be of any color or ethnic background, male or female, but each one serves us every day. John F. Kennedy said, "All men are created equal, then a few become firemen."

It only takes half a minute for a small flame to turn into a full-blown life-threatening fire. Take a stovetop incident, since cooking fires account for almost half of all home fires. A few seconds is all it takes for a pot or pan to boil over the rim, spilling flammable oil-laden contents directly onto the cooking flame or red-hot electric burner. In a few hundredths of a second grease or other fatty substances ignite into flames.

Within seconds of a flame-up, fire easily spreads. Splattered grease or oil residue on a dirty stovetop will ignite, causing flames to travel across the range. Oil residue on cooking utensils also catch fire, and other combustibles like paper towels, paper or cardboard packaging, and dry dish towels nearby will begin to smolder or burn. As the fire grows higher and hotter, more flammable objects and furnishings will ignite from spreading flames, including wooden cabinets and countertops, wallpaper, hanging baskets, and curtains. With the fire moving beyond the stovetop and other areas beginning to burn, a denser plume of scorching air and smoke rises and spreads across the ceiling.

In just a few minutes, the heat from a room fire can reach 1100 degrees Fahrenheit. As this happens, flashover occurs. Everything in the room bursts into flames—wood dining table, wood and upholstered chairs, cookbooks, curtains, and wall decorations. The oxygen in the room is virtually sucked out; glass windows shatter. Balls of fire and flames shoot out windows and doorways. The upstairs fills with thick, hot, noxious smoke and the stairwell is impassable. When you have flashover in a room, temperatures can reach up to 1,400 degrees Fahrenheit—now, all of the other rooms in the house are severely at risk.

After making it to the front of the burning home, it took me a few moments to absorb the scene. Several dozen firefighters were working frantically to suppress the raging fire that was engulfing the home. Multiple fire departments were active on the scene. It has been classified a "mutual aid" operation, which is an agreement among emergency responders to lend assistance across jurisdictional boundaries. It was chaos. I stood there frozen, not sure how to enter the fray. Just then a captain a few feet away pointed at me and yelled out, "You! Get a SCBA on, and follow these three, mount an offensive on the bravo side." A SCBA is an abbreviation for a *self-contained breathing apparatus*, a device worn by rescue workers and firefighters to provide breathable air in an IDLH—*immediately dangerous to life or health atmosphere.*

When we got to the bravo or left side of the house, a firefighter inside yelled out, "Need refills now!" Their air cylinders were depleted and had to be refilled. I was charged with this task and jumped into action. For thirty minutes I furiously refilled canisters and ran them back.

It took five fire departments from three counties to knock down all visible fire, but the house was a total loss. With refilled air tanks, we transitioned to "overhaul and salvage," which is walking through a house making sure there are no hidden fires or hot spots while trying to salvage anything of value. Protecting property is a responsibility of firefighters. Property can be irreplaceable or of high sentimental value. In some cases, contents can be more valuable than the structure itself. As I walked through the smoldering house, I recovered a few shattered and melted picture frames from the rubble, with photographs of what looked to be a mother and father, and three young children. As devastating as this fire was in terms of property damage, the fact that there was no loss of life or injuries was a victory.

Heidi greeted me in the driveway when I returned home. I stepped out of the car, still in my firefighter gear, covered in soot and grime. She stood stoically and glared at me. After brushing myself off, I looked at her and said mischievously, "I checked it out." Trying to contain it, a smile forced its way across her face, which was one part, I should beat you with a stick right now, and one part, I can't not love you.

After a long hot shower, I related the entire account to Heidi over a bowl of beef and barley stew. There was danger, risk, and peril involved in fighting this fire, but there was also courage, camaraderie, and a sense of transcendent purpose and greater good involved. This is why so many little boys and girls dream of being a firefighter. There is a noble, heroic, gutsy, hallowed, and lion-hearted essence to it.

I do not remember a whole lot from my college psychology class, but the concept of an archetype stuck with me. An archetype is a pattern of behavior that becomes a prototype that we associate with a particular symbol or kind of person. They are typically recurring motifs in literature, art, and film. For example, "the sage" is a well-known archetype. Yoda, the Oracle, Gandalf, Mr. Miyagi fit the sage archetype.

Another archetype, which is in the mind of every young boy or girl who wants to be a firefighter, is the archetype of the hero. The hero braves danger, risk, adversity, and foe to carry out a good feat, save the day, and rescue people in distress. Think Batman, Odysseus, and Joan of Arc. The typical hero is called into a risky mission. They enter an unknown world of mysteries and dangers, and must overcome trials, tribulations, adversities, and foes along the way. These battles target upon the hero's fears, worries, and doubts. The hero trusts in themselves and their cause, and courageously press forward. The mission is accomplished, and the hero returns home a transformed person.

The firefighter fits this archetype as the 'everyman' hero. We do not leap over buildings in a single bound or fly over buildings in a cape, we run into buildings that are ablaze, imperiling our lives to rescue another.

Kids and adults alike, we all cherish a hero. Not only do we love and adore heroes, but each of us also wants to be a hero. Stories of courage and bravery rouse something deeply rooted within us. We imagine ourselves with the courage to champion a great cause, brave obstacles, and danger to win a grand victory, and return home a changed and transformed person. Heroic stories remind us of who we are and wish we could be. We feel we are meant to be heroes. Comic book writer, Grant Morrison, wrote, "We love our superheroes because they refuse to give up on us. We can analyze them out of existence, kill them, ban them, mock them, and still they return, patiently reminding us of who we are and what we wish we could be."

In the Bible, the eleventh chapter of the Book of Hebrews honors those who lived their lives heroically. I have never been on a scene as a first responder chaplain that was more gruesome than the scenarios this chapter describes. It includes people who were: "tortured", "flogged", "chained and imprisoned", "thrown into fire", "stoned", "sawed in two", "killed by the sword", "destitute, persecuted and mistreated", "wandered in deserts and mountains, living in caves and in holes in the ground."

Why were they treated this way? Because they were unwilling to compromise their faith, conviction, and purpose in life. Their faith, conviction, and purpose were greater than any hardship, adversity, foe, or suffering. And for this, the writer of the Book of Hebrews said this about these heroes, "...the world was not worthy of them."

Sometimes the world feels like a burning building. Our lives can feel like being thrown into a fire. We have a few options here. We can blame and be angry with God. We can spiral down into the abyss of trying to figure out why it is happening. We can despair that life is void of all meaning, goodness, mercy, and purpose. We can become bitter, resentful, and jaded.

But there is another option. We can courageously choose to lean into our hardships and refuse to be defeated by our suffering. We can persevere in trust, believe, and hope, in the face of adversity and tragedy. We can valiantly choose to get back up after we have been knocked down, for the fifth time. We can choose to live another day or another hour, even when life feels dark and desperate. That is a hero.

Have you ever noticed that our finest moments often follow our darkest ones? 9/11 was one of the most devastating, deadliest, and despairing moments in our nation's history. Firefighters I wish I knew lost their lives or were severely injured. 343 firefighters, including a chaplain, perished in the line of duty. Firefighter Michael F. Cammarata was only 22. William M. Feehan was 72.

Mychal Fallon Judge was the chaplain to the New York City Fire Department, who lost his life. 3,000 people attended Judge's funeral Mass on September 15, 2001, at St. Francis of Assisi Church, which was presided over by Cardinal Edward Egan, the Archbishop of New York. In an interview in 1992, Mychal Judge said, "I wonder what my last hour will be. Will it be trying to help someone, trying to save a life?"

But following that dark moment in our nation's history, was one of our brightest. Our love, compassion, faith, courage, humanity, solidarity, fortitude, generosity, kindness, beauty, tenderness, resolve, and nobility were on display. In the face of 9/11 we became wounded healers, one to another. I believe Mychal Judge and many others who gave and lost their lives in that tragedy would have made the Hebrews chapter 11 list.

You know who else would make the list? Candace Lightner, who founded Mothers Against Drunk Drivers (MADD), after her 13-year-old daughter, Cari, was killed by a drunk driver. So would Richard Miles. He was wrongly convicted of a murder he did not commit and spent 15 years in prison before he was proven to be innocent. After prison he became the founder of Miles of Freedom, a non-profit organization that aids and supports individuals returning home from prison and their families. Our world is filled with everyday heroes who endure, overcome, and transcend heartache, injustice, and hardship.

You and I both know there will be hardship, adversity, loss, injustice, and affliction in this world. Each of us will be thrown into the fire of grief, heartache, and despair. None of us are exempt. But tragedies are turned into triumphs, beauty is made from ashes, hope rises from the rubble, and our moments of deepest transformation are forged in the crucible of suffering.

As the writer of Hebrews said, the world is not worthy of people like this, which means that the highest expression of what it means to be human is when we heroically lean into our darkest moments and are transformed by them. You do not have to fight fires, be faster than a speeding bullet, or see your name in a news headline to be a hero. You do not need special gear, a position, or a title, or be on some epic mission. A hero is simply someone who keeps going, keeps trusting, keeps believing, and keeps living. Christopher Reeve wrote, "A Hero is an ordinary individual who finds the strength to persevere and endure in spite of overwhelming obstacles."

Maybe "faith" is not the assurance that our lives will always make sense or that God will even make sense but putting one foot in front of the other when faith doesn't.

Here's to all the people who...

were told they were incurably bad, broken, defective and inadequate;

endured abuse and the absence of love, affirmation, validation, approval and acceptance;

have walked through personal hell multiple times;

were made to feel they were stupid, ugly and useless;

are thinking for themselves and following their truth and convictions in the face of rejection, disapproval and judgment;

wake up most days, feeling like the deck is stacked against them with insurmountable obstacles on their path;

are responsible to earn an income, raise kids and make life work without the help of a spouse or partner;

are seldom on the receiving end but never stop being kind, thoughtful and generous...

...and still here,

still pressing forward,

still putting one foot in front of the other,

still being a person of love, kindness and goodwill.

Thank you for being you. Thank you for persevering. Thank you for your heart. Thank you for being an inspiration to others who wonder if or how they will get through.

You are my hero.

CHAPTER 6

"HE'S THE GUY!"

It is one of the oldest courtroom scenes in America: a prosecutor in a criminal trial asks a key witness if he sees the person who committed the crime anywhere in the room. There is a portentous pause, filled with drama, tension, and anticipation. The witness turns and points to the defendant, as the jurors take it all in, and says, "It was him!"

I witnessed such a scene as a juror in a trial involving a man who was robbed at gunpoint for his pit bull puppies. As a volunteer firefighter, I was surprised to be chosen since the plaintiff was also a firefighter.

The firefighter plaintiff who was selling pit bull puppies agreed to meet a potential buyer in a school parking lot on a Saturday afternoon. The supposed buyer approached the car with an accomplice, pulled out a shotgun, stuck it in the face of the firefighter, and demanded the puppies be handed over. The firefighter grabbed the barrel of the shotgun, wrestled it away, and the robber and accomplice ran. The accomplice was apprehended a short time later by the police, and he gave up the defendant who was later arrested.

It just so happened that the defendant's mother worked as a maid for the best defense lawyer in Austin, and he pulled out all the stops in the trial to create reasonable doubt that his client was the guy involved in the altercation.

USED TO GO TO CHURCH

The defense attorney began by citing research on the fallibility of eyewitness testimony in general. He mentioned a 2016 state supreme court decision in Connecticut, which held that witnesses cannot be asked for an in-court identification unless they knew the defendant before the crime or have already successfully identified the defendant in an out-of-court procedure, or the perpetrator's identity is not contested.

The lawyer continued with presenting a defense that included witness after witness who testified that the defendant was somewhere else at the time of the robbery. The defendant's saintly mother testified that her son was at home in bed during the time of the incident. There was an analysis of the video evidence of the police interview with the accomplice and testimony from an expert witness from Baylor University, all of which were meant to cast reasonable doubt in the minds of the jury.

The prosecutor cross-examined the defense witnesses and used his own, as well as additional evidence to prove that the defendant committed the crime. He made his case and implored the jury to render a guilty verdict. His final effort was calling the firefighter to the stand. The prosecutor asked him if he clearly remembered the person who had attempted the robbery. The firefighter responded that he could never forget the face of someone who pointed the barrel of a shotgun into his forehead. The prosecutor asked, "Is that man in this courtroom right now?" "Yes." the firefighter answered decisively. Looking to the jury, the prosecutor asked, "Could you point him out?" Without hesitation, the firefighter pointed to the defendant and emphatically exclaimed, "He's the guy!" The prosecutor asked, "Are you sure?," and the firefighter repeated himself even more forcefully, "He's the guy!!"

The firefighter was convincing with his finger pointed directly at "the guy." This left quite an impression on the jury. We deliberated the case and delivered a guilty verdict.

Later that same week I was driving to pick up my son from soccer practice, and while sitting at a traffic light, I noticed a church on the corner with a marquee that read, "If you were arrested for being a Christian, would there be enough evidence to convict you?" It was not the first time I had encountered this question, which is a common Christian thought experiment meant to provoke people to judge their religious holiness and devotion.

The term "Christian" is commonly used to distinguish a person's religious affiliation; a Christian is to Christianity what a Muslim is to Islam, what a Jew is to Judaism, and so on. Technically, the ending "-ian" means "belonging to the party of." Some believe that originally the term "Christian" reflected a derisive sentiment that was referring to those who belonged to Jesus' party or sect and did not acknowledge the emperor of Rome. In more practical terms, the modern use of the word "Christian" is meant to convey someone whose beliefs about God are derived from the person, life, and teachings of Jesus.

However, it is curious that Christians are particularly well-known for their theological doctrines and beliefs, and yet Jesus rarely, if ever, taught theology. Jesus' ideas about God were surprisingly simple and personal, and he typically used everyday parables, stories, and ideas to convey spiritual truth. Christians are also most notably known for attending church, yet Jesus never started a church, he actually criticized the structures, hierarchies, and professional religious class of his religious tradition. Modern Christianity places the highest value on believing, studying, venerating, and defending the Bible, yet Jesus challenged people to adopt universal values such as love, compassion, justice, virtue, brotherhood, service, generosity, and respect for the dignity of all human beings.

Christians are notorious for their certainty about the afterlife destinations of heaven and hell, yet Jesus declared that his kingdom is present now, and did not seem to have any definitive explanation about an afterlife heaven or hell. The official creeds most associated with the Christian Church such as the Apostles' Creed and Nicene Creeds, are replete with theological and philosophical explanations about God, salvation, afterlife, and the Trinity, but do not contain any of Jesus' words, statements, or sayings.

Despite all these conflicts, there is no debate that Jesus Christ is at the center of Christianity. The literal meaning of the word "Islam" is "surrender," meaning submission to the will of God. It is a very direct term about one's relationship to Allah. The term "Judaism" is literally translated as "Judah," an ethno-religious term that signifies the Kingdom of Israel. But at the heart of Christianity, even its name, is the person history knows as Jesus Christ. "He is the guy" at the center of it all.

But who is he? Perhaps no person in history has been the subject of so much controversy and debate. It began two thousand years ago, when religious and political powers conspired to brutally execute him. Virtually all modern scholars of antiquity agree that Jesus existed historically. After that point, agreement is difficult to find; opinions about the life and message of Jesus differ sharply.

My own understanding of Jesus has been a long and winding journey. I grew up attending church and first learned the Sunday School Jesus. With every head bowed and every eye closed, I said the Sinner's Prayer and accepted Jesus as my Lord and Savior. Jesus was my golden ticket to heaven when I died. Years later I went to divinity school and earned a degree in Jesus, graduating with airtight and unfailing evangelical theology. Then in professional Christian ministry I extolled church Jesus. As the pastor of a congregation I stressed the importance of church attendance, membership, tithing, and serving...in the name of Jesus.

As a first responder chaplain, I discovered something curious. Whenever I introduced myself as a chaplain, people would immediately go to church, religion or God in their thinking and reaction. As mentioned, a common response was, "I used to go to church." In other cases, people would either divulge that they were not a religious person, or they would identify with a particular religious affiliation, "I was raised Catholic" or "I'm Presbyterian." Often as a chaplain, a person will request that I pray to God on their behalf or about their situation. But I cannot remember a time when Jesus specifically ever came up. Church, yes. Religion, yes. Prayer, yes. Bible, yes. God, yes.

But not Jesus.

Doesn't that seem strange? The person of Jesus is at the center of Christianity, even by name, but he hardly comes up. Christianity is classified as the largest world religion with 2.5 billion adherents. And yet Jesus claimed he did not come to start a new religion. In fact, Jesus was a one-man wrecking crew in opposition to the religious establishment. He distrusted, dismissed, disobeyed, disrespected, and denounced virtually every facet of organized religion.

So, if not to establish the Christian religion, then what was the point of Jesus?

In the Gospel of John there is a story where one of Jesus' followers requests that Jesus orchestrate a supernatural experience in which the full measure of God is miraculously revealed. Disappointed by his request, Jesus answers, "You've been with me all this time, Philip, and you still don't understand? To see me is to see the Father."

The point of Jesus was to reveal God. However, who Jesus revealed God to be, was diametrically opposed to the exacting, condemning, wrathful, distant, detached, and sanctimonious God of religion.

The life Jesus lived–loving the unlovable, forgiving the unforgivable, welcoming the dispossessed, befriending the abandoned, remembering the forgotten, protecting the powerless, uplifting the downtrodden, comforting the brokenhearted, defending the victimized–this life was the revelation of God. Whenever, wherever, or through who-ever this spirit is expressed, God is revealed.

A person will discover many different understandings and explana-tions about God in the countless religions, philosophies, belief sys-tems, spiritualities, creeds, doctrines, and faith communities through-out history and the world. But the reason the person known as Jesus is profoundly significant to humankind is because when it comes to knowing who or what God really is, "he's the guy."

In a nutshell, Christianity according to Jesus is that God is not some abstract theological construction somewhere distant in the sky that you relate to through the explanations, stipulations, obligations, checklists, rules, structures, and clerics of religion. Go into your heart and your humanity, go into yourself to the depths from which your life flows, access what you most deeply know and have always known. Love, mercy, compassion, caring, grace, goodwill, kindness, solidarity, virtue, courage–this is the highest truth, this is the ultimate reality, this is God. This was the point of Jesus.

I came to the realization in my spiritual journey that everything I really need to know about God is adequately depicted through the stories passed down and recorded about the person and life of Jesus.

Sometimes it seems like the world is a colossal courtroom and everyday God is on trial for the hardships, tragedies, and sufferings of humankind. There are those who blame God, and others who defend God. Some have faith; some have doubt. For some people, the answers and explanations of religion work, for others they make no sense at all. As a first responder chaplain, I have encountered some of the most grim, gruesome, heartrending, despairing, and devastating moments in people's lives. If I was called to the stand and interrogated about how I explained God in light of all this, I would just stand, raise my hand, clear my voice, point my finger at the man from Nazareth on the back row and say firmly, "He's the guy!"

CHAPTER 7

MOMS DON'T DIE

Moms don't die.

It is a rule.

Every human person owes his or her life to a mother. She endures the pain of childbirth to deliver you into the world. Moms do it all. They were multitasking long before it ever became a recognizable skill. Motherhood is a thankless job, but it is a profoundly necessary one. Perhaps no saying is more quoted than, "The hand that rocks the cradle is the hand that rules the world." Moms are always there. They are invincible and indestructible. What on earth could ever be compared to the power of a mother's love? You need your mother.

No, mothers are not supposed to die. Especially not if it is your mother when you are a child or adolescent. People die every day but when you are a kid, not your mom.

One of the worst moments in my work as a chaplain was the day that I had to inform a teenager that his mother had died. Her tragic death happened two days before his high school graduation.

It was a blithe spring day as I was out playing a round of golf with a few friends, when I received a call that I was urgently needed at San Ramon Regional Hospital. A forty-two-year-old mother of two teens had suffered a major cardiac event.

On my way, I was filled in with more details. The mother's teenage son came home after school to find his mother unconscious on the living room floor. He immediately called 911 and the dispatcher instructed him to perform CPR. Try to picture this harrowing scene—a teenage boy performing CPR on his mother to save her life.

When the paramedics arrive, they jump into action taking every measure to revive this mom, as the son looks on. She is quickly lifted onto a stretcher and placed in the ambulance with her son, and rushed to the hospital, sirens and lights blazing. The boy's brother, and the woman's father and siblings were notified. It was a close-knit family who lived near each other, and they were all at the hospital just minutes after the ambulance arrived.

Entering the ER, I was told that the woman's two sons and other family members were distraught and had assembled in the waiting room. Making my way down the hallway in that direction, I passed the patient room with curtains drawn open and saw the mother. One of our firefighters was sweating profusely while continuing CPR on her, as doctors and nurses were doing everything within their power to resuscitate her.

I learned later that this firefighter refused to let anyone take over doing CPR and was completely consumed in the moment to bring her back. Even after she flatlined and it was clear she had not lived, they had to pull him away from her. Saving lives is not a job. It is personal. This firefighter had a mother. It's a rule. Moms don't die. Not on his watch.

But this one did.

Before I walked into the waiting room to meet the family, the doctor pronounced her dead. Knowing who I was, he requested that I join him to inform the family.

When you notify someone that a loved one has died, as I have done many times, you know that the words you speak will forever change the course of life for those who hear them.

As a chaplain who has worked with military families, and been in countless hospitals, drug rehab centers, bereavement centers, hospices, and prisons, I have seen too many instances where well-intentioned health care workers, church members, clergy, and friends say unhelpful things to people when a death has occurred.

A nurse comes into the room of a weeping mother who has lost her baby and tells her, "It is all right; don't cry. You can have another child." The mother feels like she has been told it is not okay to feel her sorrow and grief; to snap out of it because there are better days ahead.

The church member says to a person grieving a lost loved one, "They are in a better place." The griever may believe this too, but in that moment, they want them desperately to be in this place.

When tragedy strikes, the pastor doubles down on the sovereignty of God. The griever is made to feel wrong for naturally questioning, resisting and grieving their loss. The people who say such things are often uncomfortable by the griever's pain and want to soften the devastation by saying something.

I find it curious that religious people are often the most reluctant to allow people to feel the full force of their sadness and grief in the face of loss. The short but powerful Bible verse, "Jesus wept" depicts the humanity of Jesus in the form of deep anguish and sorrow. The Bible often speaks of God as experiencing sadness and grief.

There are two important aspects of informing a person of the death of a loved one. The first is that you state it factually. When you notify someone that a loved one has died, you do not mince words. You do not try to mask it. You do not substitute words for "died" with phrases like "is no longer with us" or "didn't make it." You say it compassionately but plainly—"your mother has died," "your daughter has died." I have delivered this news countless times, "I'm so sorry to tell you that your (son, daughter, mother, father, wife, husband) has died."

Uttering these words to this family, I can feel each syllable heavy in my vocal cords and exiting my mouth, as my lungs force them outward. On the other end of that grim utterance is shock, heartache, devastation, anguish, and despair.

The second critical component of delivering the news to someone that a loved one had died, is allowing them to feel and express their emotions. There are no rules or scripts for grief. Reactions I have seen, range from stoic disbelief to outbursts of emotion. Sometimes the response is a quiet acceptance, while other situations involve an eruption of emotional volatility. At times there is relief, other times despair; sometimes silent tears of relinquishment, and other times screams of denial and protest from the pit of their soul.

As a chaplain, I refrain from making any attempt to correct or address the expressions of grief unless someone is a threat to them-selves or others. I do not try to theologize, spiritualize or bright side it. This is not the time for the "power of positive thinking."

I have learned over these years of encountering people in their darkest moments, that it is necessary to allow them any feelings they might have. Rule #1 for a chaplain is not to meddle or usurp the expression of emotions, however good your intentions might be.

Jesus is the quintessential first responder chaplain. He did not God-talk people's suffering. Jesus tasted the depths of heartache, grief, and despair himself. A recurring motif in the Bible is the "suffering servant", most notably described in the fifty-third chapter of the Old Testament Book of Isaiah, which is viewed as a prophesy about Jesus, particularly the words, "He was a man of suffering and familiar with pain." In the New Testament Book of Hebrews, the writer asserts that what most qualified Jesus to care for people's souls was the experience of his own human suffering.

The picture of Jesus given in the gospels is one of a wounded healer. He did not stand outside the reality of human suffering unscathed, offering a clean holy hand. Jesus gave himself to people from inside the real world of human loss, grief, and sorrow. He reached out with a heart of deep compassion and true empathy, forged in the crucible of his own suffering. Jesus wept in the face of human pain.

The Christian church has given Jesus many high and lofty titles, but the one Jesus most favored for himself was "Son of Man," which is a term expressing human solidarity. Studying the life of Jesus, I saw how skillfully he navigated the adversities and afflictions of the human journey. He did not live in denial or suppress the natural emotional agony all human beings feel in heartbreak and tragedy. But neither was Jesus swallowed whole by the suffering of human existence. Jesus offered a middle way: not to deny, downplay, or explain away our suffering, nor to be conquered or shackled by it.

Receiving the news that this mother had died; the family was shocked and devastated. Every death of a loved one is difficult, but for different reasons. In this case, this mother showed no signs of poor health, and was perfectly well and happy when her teenage son went to school that morning. When a loved one has been seriously ill for an extended period and dies, as heartrending as this can be, you are likely to feel more prepared for it. But in this instance with her unexpected death, the family was blindsided and steamrolled by calamity.

I wondered about the father of these two boys. It was strange that the entire family was present, except him. I learned from a family relative at the hospital that the father passed away only a year earlier after a long drawn out battle with ALS. I do not know of a more humbling and unforgiving disease, both for the individual and the family who see the agonizing decline of their loved one, slowly succumbing to death.

As the family was grieving, I went over to the father of the woman, a man in his late 60's. He seemed to be what we call around here "good people"—genuine, plain-speaking, unpretentious; a loving father and grandfather. Losing a child at any age is unbearable for a parent. Parents always see their adult sons and daughters as their sweet babies, never letting go of their tender and protective love of them.

He described his daughter as an extraordinary woman and devoted wife and mother. She had made heroic sacrifices to provide care to her dying husband up until his death a year earlier. He told me how the boys, especially the older one had an exceedingly difficult time dealing with their father's death. And now this.

Can you imagine losing a father and mother in the same year as a teenager?

Sadly, this is not the only such occasion I have seen as a chaplain. A few weeks prior to this incident, I sat with a 15-year-old boy who found his father deceased in the backyard after getting up in the morning to go to school. His mom passed away two years earlier at the same home. He was an only child, now with both parents deceased.

There was another case when a 5-year-old little girl, who now is an adult friend, was the sole survivor of a head on collision caused by a drunk driver. The little girl lost both her parents and two siblings in the fatal crash. No doubt there are readers of this book who lost their mom or dad, maybe both, when they were young.

This father standing before me in the ER waiting room was deeply concerned about his grandsons losing both parents while also feeling shattered by the sudden loss of his beloved daughter. Family members were weeping and clutching each other, as firefighters, paramedics, ER doctors and nurses looked on, feeling the full brunt of this tragic death, despite their valiant effort.

Dad looked me square in the eye and asked without any anger but with deep sadness and disbelief, "Why would God let this happen?"

My heart sank. After all this family had been through, why would God take the woman who was loved, kind, giving, and so important to these two boys?

Why?

Why would God seemingly orphan these kids with no father or mother?

Why?

Moms don't die.

I understood their "why" question, and the depth of feelings enmeshed in it. I have asked and felt this same question. There is some part of me that asks and feels it on every call I respond to as a first responder chaplain. Why? Why this? Why them? Why now?

When faced with a tragedy that befalls others, especially the young, innocent, or seemingly undeserving, there is a feeling of injustice, unfairness, even betrayal. In an instant, the well-ordered world of an all-powerful and loving God working out his perfect plan, is turned upside down on its head. Where is said God in situations such as this? How can you square up an all-powerful and loving God with two boys having their mother and father randomly and fatefully ripped from their lives?

My life as a chaplain involves being asked a long list of questions for which I do not have good answers. Some of the answers do not sound half bad when you are sitting all comfy, blessed and holy in church, far removed from traumatic loss and despair, and the preacher is weaving together Bible verses in explanations that seem irrefutable. But Sunday sermon reasoning is woefully inadequate and irrelevant for these two boys wailing in the ER waiting room, who just heard that their mother has died.

These boys will never stop loving their mother. They will never forget her. They will always know her face. But she will always be dead. It will never be okay that they lost their mother. Moms are not supposed to die. Nobody can intervene and make it right and nobody will. Nobody can take it back with silence or push it away with words. Nobody can protect you from your suffering.

Years ago, as a young and inexperienced chaplain, I tried talking my way through these tragedies by pretending I had comforting and assuring insights. So often people feel their job is to make people who are hurting feel better. It is not. It is more a matter of bearing witness. To be with them, share their pain with them, and allow them their feelings, every single one of them—that is a true gift that is more priceless than words can say.

Grief is woven into the fabric of the human experience. Sorrow is not sickness or a lack of faith, it is a normal and natural occurrence in daily life. If anyone tells you some form of get over it, move on, or rise above, you can let them go. If anyone avoids you amidst loss or pretends like it did not happen, or disappears from your life, you can let them go. If anyone tells you that all is not lost, that it happened for a reason, that you will become better because of your grief, you can let them go.

Eventually I learned that serving people on the scene of human suffering is bearing witness with compassion, acceptance, humility, respect, and faith.

"Faith" in what? You may ask.

Faith that feelings of mourning, sorrow, anger, fear, heartache, anguish, and despair are what it means to be human in the face of loss and tragedy.

Faith that there is a grief and healing process that a human being can walk through. There is no real formula for grieving. No two losses are the same. Each loss stands on its own and inflicts a unique kind of pain. No one can fully know another's suffering. Grief and loss bring a sudden halt to business as usual. The pain comes and goes and comes and goes. You do not pass one stage, scratch it off your list, and graduate onto the next. It is choppy and messy and nonlinear. Grief is visceral, not reasonable; the howling at the center is raw and real. Grief comes in waves, convulsions, sudden trepidations that weaken the knees, blind the eyes, and obliterate the dailiness of life.

The experience of loss itself does not have to be the defining moment of our lives. Instead, the defining moment can be our response to the loss. We are capable of absorbing loss into our lives. Frederick Buechner wrote, "Even the saddest things can become, once we have made peace with them, a source of wisdom and strength for the journey that still lies ahead."

Grief and loss are often the catalyst for a person to take inventory of their lives, to reconsider priorities, determine new directions, and clarify what truly matters most in life. Faith believes that just as there will always be experiences of pain and suffering on the human journey, there will also be joy, beauty, peace, grace, and gratitude.

In a moment of human suffering, the answer to the question "What would Jesus do?" includes having a crisis of faith and feeling betrayed by God. Jesus was rejected, abandoned, humiliated, brutalized and left to die alone on a cross suspended between two criminals. He had his own "why" question, "My God, my God, why have you forsaken me?" Every person who has endured catastrophic loss and suffering, understands these words of Jesus. We feel forsaken—forsaken by God, by life, by time, by our hopes and dreams. In these dark moments of our lives, we are supposed to feel all of that.

In the ER I offered to say a prayer for the family, and the father at once expressed that he would appreciate me doing so. The emergency room staff had prepared the mother's body in a separate room, and we all gathered around her in a circle. We stood silently for a few moments as I glanced around the room, noticing this collection of hurting human beings. There were two teenage boys who lost their mom, just a year after the death of their dad. A father who would never again hug his daughter. Siblings who were forced to say good-bye to a sister they loved. Scattered throughout the room were first responders and ER doctors, all with heavy hearts from the tragic death of this mother.

And then there was me. The chaplain. The chaplain with no good answers. The chaplain with no explanation to make all this go away or even make it understandable. But a chaplain who had faith that this tragedy would not be the last chapter.

Jesus once said, "For where two or three are gathered in my name, there I am in the midst of them." Gathered in a circle in that ER room where hearts were aching, tears were falling, sorrow was piercing, and grief was crushing, we were standing on holy ground. Jesus, the suffering servant, and wounded healer knew firsthand that ache, those tears, the sorrow, and grief that pierces the soul. Loss is the heartbreaking club to which we all eventually belong.

Every person's story begins with a mother. She carries you in her body for nine months, and in her soul for a lifetime. We never lose our mother entirely, a part of her is knitted into the very fabric of who we are and goes with us.

It is true after all.

Moms don't die.

CHAPTER 8

ODE TO TIM EBERT

A 49-year-old woman stood in the parking lot of an upscale business park, holding a gun to her head. The woman had been ensnared in the grips of depression and was particularly distraught when she left that morning to take her dog to the vet. Hours passed and she had not returned home. Her husband became increasingly concerned. Using his iPhone tracking app, he pinpointed her location at a nearby business park, which was odd; she did not work there. He immediately called 911, giving the police her location and type of car.

Last year in the US there were 24,000 people who took their own lives with a gun. The US leads the world in gun-related suicides. A major cause of suicide is mental illness, very commonly depression. Research has consistently shown a strong link between suicide and depression. People feeling suicidal are overwhelmed by painful emotions and see death as the only way out, losing sight of the fact that suicide is a permanent "solution" to a temporary state. Most people who try to kill themselves but live, later say they are glad they did not die. The woman with the gun in the parking lot had suffered a series of significant health-related problems and was forced to leave her job. She became increasingly depressed but never sought professional treatment.

When the officers arrived, they spotted her standing near her parked car under some trees. From the information relayed from dispatch, they knew that she was unstable and possibly suicidal. These are tense situations for law enforcement. They can never rule out the probability that the subject might become a threat to others or initiate a "suicide by cop" scenario in which the suicidal individual deliberately behaves in a threatening manner, with intent to provoke a lethal response.

A typical law enforcement strategy for preventing a suicide is to first allow the person to have their physical space, not moving too close too soon, and avoiding sudden movements and alarmist attitudes or behavior. Officers are trained to calmly engage the individual with acceptance, empathy, and concern, and encourage the person to talk. The hope is that a conversation can ensue about a solution to the problem the person is experiencing and the officers' willingness to help. Meanwhile, a police officer in this scenario is always plotting how to remove access to any lethal means of self-harm, in this case the Smith & Wesson revolver that the woman was holding.

After an initial exchange of words, the woman became increasingly distressed and stopped talking. One of the officers asked if he could come a little closer to converse more easily with her. The woman asked that he give her just a minute to collect herself, and then suddenly she pointed the barrel of the gun into her chest and pulled the trigger. They quickly rendered aid at that point to no avail; it was a fatal shot.

I was initially asked to meet the husband at the scene. But when it was discovered that the woman was being transported to the hospital, I was redirected to meet him there. At the hospital I informed him that his wife had shot herself and did not survive, despite every attempt to save her. He was not surprised that his wife had attempted suicide, but he was in shock that she had died.

As a first responder chaplain, I am confronted regularly by mental health issues that relate to tragic situations such as suicide. There are also many mental health problems that affect the first responders who are summoned daily to the frontlines of gruesome and horrific events. Consider the traumatic situation with the woman in the parking lot. Her suicide was directly related to a mental health crisis. Then there were the police officers who tried but failed to save the woman. They watched her pull the trigger, offered emergency medical aid to her hemorrhaging body, and saw her gasping for her last breaths before she died. These officers have likely been involved in hundreds of loss-of-life scenarios grislier than this.

First and foremost, my work as a first responder chaplain is to tend to the emotional and mental wellbeing of first responders in EMS, Fire, Law Enforcement and Dispatch agencies—both on-scene and behind the scenes. These heroes sometimes need help and support. It is estimated that close to 40 percent of first responders develop behavioral health conditions including, but not limited to, depression, substance abuse, and post-traumatic stress disorder (PTSD). A police officer or firefighter is more likely to die by suicide than by being killed in the line of duty. In law enforcement, the estimates suggest between 125 and 300 police officers commit suicide every year. In 2018, 167 law enforcement officers tragically took their own lives, and that number is projected to rise considerably.

In my personal experience growing up in the Christian church and later becoming a professional clergyman myself, I must admit that the church has failed to adequately address the subject of mental health. Christianity has a bad habit of diminishing the body in favor of elevating the spirit or soul. The Western church's thinking on spirit and flesh imagines that the body is an inferior attachment to an idealized, spiritual soul. This has created a divide between body and soul, resulting in a focus on the care of the soul, with little attention given to how the health of mind, body, and soul are integrated. This has not only created bad religion but has meant that Christians overlook the prevalence of mental illness in their churches.

In the routine life of a church community, those with mental health difficulties are often further marginalized by behavioral and spiritual requirements that through faith one should get better, find happiness, serve not be served, or be disciplined to a collective form of worship. Too often, Christians are not encouraged to look for counseling or other mental health services, but instead told to pray harder and have more faith. The silent stigma of mental health issues in the church relate to the false perception that they are an indication of weakness, spiritual immaturity, lack of faith and devotion, and a failed relationship with God.

That is not to say that spirituality does not play a role in a person's wholeness and wellbeing. Of course you would hope that a person would reap the mental and emotional benefits of applying true spiritual wisdom, being in a faith community of genuine, caring, authentic, vulnerable, and meaningful relationships, and knowing that God loves and supports you unconditionally. That would be wonderful. However, I suspect that all those people who "used to go to church" did not quite have that experience.

Even if they had, the fact is that you cannot pray away a mental health condition, unless "prayer" means believing that God supports and goes with you as you seek mental health support you need. It is a false notion to believe a mental health condition is "in God's hands" unless this means that seeking counseling or other forms of mental health support or treatment is a way of properly utilizing the mind God gave us to respond skillfully to situations as they require. The Bible verse that is often paraphrased as, "God never gives you more than you can handle" does not mean a truly spiritual person should be able to work out mental health issues on their own. Depression is not a "spiritual problem." Mental illness is not punishment for one's sins.

There is a story in the Gospel of John when Jesus comes upon a man who has been blind since birth. Jesus' disciples asked him whether it was the man's parents or the man himself who had sinned to bring this condition upon him. Jesus said that neither the man nor his parents sinned to cause his blindness. Jesus turned the conversation away from their misguided conjecture about the cause of the man's physical condition and focused on facilitating a solution.

Jesus made a mud pack from dirt and spit and carefully applied it to the man's eyes as part of the healing process. Perhaps Jesus knew there was something chemically in the dirt that would stimulate the man's eyesight. It did not happen as an instantaneous miraculous healing; the man was required to go to a nearby pool of water and wash the mud pack from his eyes.

The church must learn to apply matters of mental health into this Jesus story. Imagine it this way. Jesus is attending a church Sunday school class and the group start discussing an absent church member who is afflicted with depression, PTSD, Bipolar Disorder, Borderline Personality Disorder, Anorexia Nervosa, or substance addiction. The Sunday school teacher says that with enough faith and prayer this person can be healed. He further explains the importance of being right with God so as not to allow sin or demonic influences to affect their minds. The Sunday school teacher rattles off a few Bible verses about how nothing is impossible with God, and shares that he had requested the church elders to organize a gathering to pray over this person and anoint him with oil. He cites a verse from the Book of Exodus, which says, "Worship the Lord your God, and his blessing will be on your food and water. I will take sickness away from among you and restore you to health."

The conversation is bantering along and suddenly Jesus stands up and addresses the class. He tells them that this person's mental health affliction is not a spiritual deficiency that can be resolved through faith, prayer, oil, or religious devotion. He says to the group that he can facilitate this person's healing. So Jesus drives to this individual's house and has a conversation with them, compassionately sharing that their affliction can be addressed, in this case not with a mud pack of dirt and spit, but by understanding that there is no shame and it is the proper response to seek mental health support and treatment. Jesus encourages them to take this step, which they do, and they receive the help they need to address their problem.

If God uses medical doctors to restore one's physical health through doctors and modern medicine, why would God not address and restore mental health issues through licensed professional counselors, psychotherapists, psychiatrists, and various treatments including medication?

I wonder how many first responders attend a church or religious community that silently stigmatize seeking professional mental health support, services, and treatment? Was the woman who took her life in that parking lot a victim of this misguided stigma?

The World Health Organization found that between 30 and 80 percent of people with mental health issues do not seek treatment. This includes 50 percent of people with bipolar disorder, 55 percent of people with PTSD disorder, 56 percent of people with major depression, and a stunning 78 percent of people with a substance addiction disorder.

One of the most significant ways I am a chaplain to first responders is to encourage them to seek professional mental health services when needed, and to know there is no shame in doing so. I consider some of my greatest triumphs as a chaplain to be those times when I succeeded in motivating a police officer, firefighter, or paramedic to seek professional mental health support. For me, this is doing God's work.

On February 1, 2019, volunteer firefighter, Tim Ebert, died by suicide. I learned this from a national firefighter website I frequent. Tim suffered from depression, which no one was aware of. Speaking to the media, his Fire Chief said, "From what everyone knows of Tim and our experiences of him, we definitely would not have suspected anything from him. He didn't seem depressed or anything. He usually had a smile on his face. He was a happy-go-lucky guy who wanted to help others."

Tim actively attended his local church. I wonder if church members knew of his depression. How many people with mental health difficulties and disorders suffer in silence? How many times was Tim superficially asked in church how he was doing, and he gave the automated response, "Fine." Too many people in churches do not feel safe to be vulnerable about their real struggles. What if someone had told Tim that running into a burning building to save a life was a brave and heroic act, and so was choosing to seek professional mental health support and treatment for depression? What if he had been told that seeing a therapist was not an indication of a lack of faith, but an expression of it?

Henry Wadsworth Longfellow, "Every man has his secret sorrows which the world knows not." As a first responder chaplain, I have encountered catastrophic distress and trauma at the tragic scenes I am called to. But there is a distress and trauma that happens inside a person that is silent, and you do not see. As a chaplain I often ask police officers, firefighters, and paramedics how they are doing. Any of them who know me have learned that I mean it. It is not a casual greeting or a mundane question you just say for an automated response. I really want to know how they are doing inside, mentally, psychologically, emotionally. I consider it to be one of the greatest gifts I offer them as a chaplain. Asking the question, meaning it, and being a safe person with whom they can be honest.

Jesus once approached a woman at a water well who was having her own inner crisis. She had an addiction to unhealthy relationships and had withdrawn and isolated herself from others. Jesus knew this woman was suffering but she would not divulge her inner turmoil to Jesus. Instead, she tried to wrangle Jesus into a religious conversation about the most sacred site at which to worship God. Jesus responded by saying that where you worship is inconsequential, and that what matters is that you approach God "in spirit and in truth." In other words, Jesus told the woman that the proper connecting place with God is always the truth of what lies within you. God just wants you to be honest, whatever that is.

God looks at each of us and asks the question, "How are you doing?" God asks because God truly wants to know. God does not want an automated response and can handle whatever the answer is. However you respond to the question, God accepts and loves you. God does not look upon you with judgment and disappointment, but with compassion and tenderness.

Maybe the people who "used to go to church" never learned this.

CHAPTER 9

ON LOSING YOUR CHRISTMAS LIST

It was Christmas, and I was beholding a holiday spectacle of neatly wrapped and colorful presents. There were scarlet red boxes with shiny gold bows, gifts wrapped with glittery snowflake paper and white lace ribbons, presents in candy cane peppermint stripes, packages in brown craft paper with festive yarn creations attached, and some that displayed words like peace, love, hope, joy, and Jesus. I was taking it all in—a festive visual gala with hundreds of perfect packages that sparkled, glistened, and glowed with Christmas.

It was not a Christmas party, holiday gathering, or community event. I was standing in the middle of freeway I680, one of the busiest freeways in the Bay Area, where hundreds of Christmas presents were strewn and scattered over four lanes from a multiple-vehicle collision. The accident included a US Postal Service truck carrying Christmas packages that overturned on its side at a high rate of speed, skidding across the freeway, and slamming into a large freeway signpost. The front cab was wrapped around the post entrapping the driver, with both his legs torn from his body below the waist.

The pressure on his torso and hip from the crumpled steel of his cab frame pinched his circulation, which kept him from bleeding to death. Paramedics and firefighters worked relentlessly at this insuperable and time-consuming extrication, while the driver was screaming in agony and pleading for his life. The man was finally unbound from the vehicle and airlifted to the nearest trauma center only to succumb to his injuries despite heroic efforts to save him. It was a surreal scene to witness such carnage and gruesome suffering surrounded by sparkling Christmas presents with words like peace, joy, and Jesus.

Just two evenings later I was called to a home where an elderly woman had suddenly died in front of her entire family, which included the woman's husband, children, and grandchildren. For them, this would be a Christmas of deep loss and grief.

The next night, I was sent by dispatch after midnight to console a little girl who had watched her parents in a vicious and violent domestic dispute. The woman doused her husband with hydrochloric acid, and he responded by brutally beating and stabbing her. The husband was airlifted to a hospital, and the wife rushed to a trauma center, both in critical condition. Only the little girl with blood splattered on her face was left at the crime scene of her home with the Christmas tree toppled and decorations trashed all over the living room floor.

Merry Christmas.

The day before the freeway incident a local 15-year-old on a skateboard was struck by a fast-moving vehicle and was put in a medically induced coma at the hospital. That same evening, I spent time with a family who's 23-year-old son suffered cardiac arrest while working at Home Depot and did not survive. I responded to another call where a 16-year-old teenager had hung himself. That same week a woman speeding down the freeway, driving under the influence, drifted off the road and struck a car on the shoulder, killing three small children.

I watched paramedics carry these little lifeless bodies away from the vehicle.

The month of December is always strenuous for first responders with the uptick of emergencies and tragedies. Researchers that analyzed 25 years of death certificates in the United States discovered that the two-week Christmas holiday is one of the deadliest. Hospital emergency rooms saw more fatalities on Christmas Day than any other day of the year. From my own twenty years of experience as a first responder chaplain, I have found this to be true. There is a spike of emergencies, tragedies, suicides, accidents, domestic violence, calamities, and casualties during the holiday season. Sacred holidays around the world such as Christmas are flashpoints for religious conflict, hatred, shootings, and violence.

Christmas commemorates the birth of Jesus. Though he was given the title of "prince of peace," Jesus was born into a distressed and violent time and place. One of the farthest corners of the Roman Empire, Judea was a land of ancient traditions and religious fervor. Decades of Roman rule had brewed deep resentment.

Jesus was born to a family from a village called Nazareth, near the Sea of Galilee. As he was growing up, Judea was collapsing into chaos. Its population had split into hostile groups, political turmoil, and religious unrest. Jesus grew up in an extremely volatile region of the world and time of history, which included the War of Varus, First Judean War, and the Archelaean Revolt.

Herod the Great was the Roman client king of Judea. History has a record of many of Herod's misdeeds, which included the murder of three of his own sons. The Gospel of Matthew claims that Herod decreed the Massacre of the Innocents, ordering the execution of all male children two years old and under in the vicinity of Bethlehem, a gruesome and bloody campaign to kill the baby Jesus. During the lifetime of Jesus his country entered a period of revolution and violence that in many ways foreshadowed the Jewish War in 66 AD, which led to the destruction of Jerusalem and its Temple. Historian of antiquity, Josephus, claimed that 1,100,000 people were killed during the siege, and 97,000 were captured and enslaved.

The distress, volatility, and violence of the world existed before the birth of Jesus, after his birth and throughout his life, and continued after Jesus' death. If you read this morning's news headlines, you will notice not much has changed. Right now, there is hatred, starvation, poverty, war, oppression, environmental destruction, racism, genocide, and a lengthy list of other maladies in our world. Every day as a first responder chaplain I encounter chaos, tribulation, and suffering. I have experienced difficulty, hardship, grief, and heartache in my own personal life, as I'm sure you have as well in some form or another.

There is quite a long history to this madness. God had barely finished declaring all things as good, before Adam and Eve decided it was not good enough and started following their ego. Paradise was abruptly and prematurely cut short when Cain drove a knife into his brother, Abel, killing him.

Merry Christmas.

Despite everything, Jesus insisted that God's perfect kingdom had already come. When he was challenged on this, he only doubled down on his claim. In fact, if you had to pin Jesus down to one primary idea that he proclaimed throughout his life it would be that the kingdom of God had arrived. There is a story in the Gospel of Luke in which Jesus is asked by a group of religious leaders when they could expect God's kingdom to come. Jesus answered that it already had. These clergymen felt humiliated. As the religious elite, how possibly could they have missed something as monumental as the coming of the kingdom of God??? They pointed out to Jesus that they could see no such kingdom.

What they were expecting as God's kingdom was political liberation from Roman rule. But Jesus had a different understanding and told them that the kingdom of God was already in their midst because it was fully intact and present within them. In other words, Jesus was teaching them that the reality of true peace, harmony, freedom, security, wellbeing, and flourishing was already present inside them. These professional preachers and Torah scholars had obviously missed that being made in the image of God meant they were lacking no good thing.

This image of God teaching was both liberating and confrontive. It was liberating to know that what we most deeply long for in our hearts and souls is already present within us, and IS us. Our underlying and true nature is composed of the essence of God. The confrontive part is the realization that waiting around for God to fix the world or airlift us out of it, is unnecessary and delusional thinking. The only reason why there is evil, hatred, war, violence, and suffering in the world is because of what we do to each other based upon our ignorance, disbelief, or denial of the truth of who we are. Humanity is to blame.

In the New Testament Book of James, this truth is deconstructed in an instructive way. James writes, "Why do you fight and quarrel? It is because your feelings are fighting inside of you. That is why you fight. You want something but you cannot get it. Then you kill. You want something very much and cannot get it. So you quarrel and fight." Do you see it? The discord, disharmony, division, and hostility in the world is a manifestation of greed, anger, envy, bitterness, resentment, and jealousy within ourselves. Humanity is to blame.

It was quite inventive for the church to turn the personification of evil into a literal being that we scapegoat for our problems and lets us off the hook from taking responsibility for the condition of our world. The notion of "spiritual warfare" is too often a cover for not getting our acts together and living as we could. Are the dark realities of our world simply the result of Satan and demons? You, me, us, we… are to blame. We started it, we perpetuate it, we choose it, but we can stop. We can fix it if we want to. The inconvenient truth we do not like is that we are responsible for the mess of the world. There is nothing or no one to blame except ourselves and our spiritual ignorance. We do not have to be doing this. We are free to choose differently. I don't buy the "devil made me do it" excuse.

We are good at making excuses for the condition our world and pretending we do not have the capacity to change it. People want Jesus to save the world because we do not have the guts to save it ourselves. Too often, religion is an impediment to taking responsibility for the world by telling us that we are weak and powerless on our own. The point of Jesus was never that he was going to save the world, but to point us to the power and authority to do so inside ourselves. Jesus leads us who follow into the realm of love, grace and joy which is saving the world now. That kingdom of God's reign is at hand.

People often wonder why God allows so much suffering and hardship in the world. Instead we should be wondering why we do. Religion cannot solve this dilemma. Religion creates a litany of rules, rituals, doctrines, and practices that only serve to create an artificial standard of righteousness to make us feel better about ourselves. Jesus exposed the bankruptcy of religion in his Sermon on the Mount. He said the standard of holiness is not abstaining from an act of murder, like Cain murdering Abel. Jesus said true holiness is to hold no malevolent thoughts, harmful intentions, or ill-will against another human being. That is God's kingdom—the absence of all such hatred, and the presence of love, compassion, peace, goodness, benevolence, joy, generosity, harmony, and goodwill.

The central message of Jesus was, "Repent for the kingdom of God has come." The conventional religious understanding of these words of Jesus could be paraphrased as follows, "The final reckoning is near, it's time to get right with God." This flawed interpretation is largely based upon the unfortunate translation of a Greek word, which was transcribed as "repent" in English. "Repent" usually means to turn away from one's sinful ways or else be subject to the judgement and wrath of God. However, the actual Greek word "metanoia" literally means "beyond the mind." In other words, it means turning toward a new understanding of something in a completely different light and to see something in a way you have never seen before.

In other words, Jesus was saying that God's kingdom will always be hidden from us as long as we think of it as a reality that God will download into our circumstances or beam us up into heaven though miraculous intervention. One of the profound insights of Jesus was that it is not necessary to escape or vacate this world to find true peace, and wellbeing. He proclaims that we can turn away to a new way of understanding humanity and ourselves as God's children.

Jesus challenged people instead to see the kingdom of God as a fully intact and accessible reality within ourselves, and one we could birth into our world through our mindsets, attitudes, words, actions, choices, and decisions. Being made in the image of God means we also share in the ability to create worlds of harmony, peace, and beauty. There is a supernatural element which plays a consistent role in our spirituality which, even though profoundly mysterious, is at work in our lives.

Christmas celebrates the birth of Jesus into the world. The rightful way to honor this sacred remembrance is by giving birth to his vision of the kingdom of God through our daily lives. Jesus lived and died for this vision and taught that when he was gone that the spirit of this vision and the power to complete would be alive in our hearts.

Our world will always include some hardships and difficulties. There are natural disasters, illness and disease, accidents and misfortunes, and death, loss, and grief. The factors that cause and contribute to these occasions are often outside our control. Imagine how different our world would be if all hatred, envy, greed, malice, hostility, and ill-will were vanquished, and replaced with love, compassion, goodness, generosity, kindness, accord, and goodwill. Every day we blame God, Satan or others for the evils and tragedies in our world, but what if we got more interested in the suffering we ourselves are causing every day.

Driving home that December evening from the freeway melee, scattered Christmas presents, and the gruesome trauma of that truck driver, Christmas songs were playing on the radio. I680 is typically a traffic nightmare, even without the backup from the freeway collision. I kept the Christmas songs going in hopes of a holiday mood change. It seems like there is a standard package of holiday songs that radio stations always play. I think I heard them all. Let's see: "All I Want for Christmas is You" by Mariah Carey; "Rockin Around the Christmas Tree" by Brenda Lee; "Jingle Bell Rock" by Bobby Helms; "A Holly Jolly Christmas" by Burl Ives; "Little Saint Nick" by the Beach Boys, and an assortment of celebrity Christmas songs sung by anyone ranging from Bruce Springsteen, Taylor Swift, Justin Bieber, and Beyoncé.

But sitting there in a sea of unmoving traffic, an old Amy Grant Christmas song came on entitled, "Grown Up Christmas List". You have probably heard it. The song recalls how we as children would create a Christmas wish list of the special gifts we hoped Santa would deliver on Christmas day. The lyricist continues by stating that although they had outgrown their childhood fantasies of Santa Claus, flying reindeer, and toys dragged down a chimney, they still carry a different kind of wish list in their heart—a grown up Christmas list. The lyrics read,

So here's my lifelong wish

My grown-up Christmas list
Not for myself but for a world in need
No more lives torn apart
That wars would never start
And time would heal all hearts
And everyone would have a friend
And right would always win
And love would never end, no
This is my grown-up Christmas list
This is my only lifelong wish
This is my grown-up Christmas list

Those lyrics pierced my heart. I realized sitting there in 1680 grid-lock that I might have lost my grown-up Christmas list somewhere back there amidst the tragedies, hardships, and heartaches I encountered over many years as a first responder chaplain. If you are not careful you can become jaded, weary of heart, detached, and even lose faith in the sentiments that sparkled on those scattered Christmas presents—peace, hope, joy, Jesus.

Maybe somewhere in life you lost your grown-up Christmas list too. You may not find it in the morning news headlines or even in all our theological explanations for the suffering we find in our world. But maybe we can find and recover it inside our own hearts. Jesus said that was the place to find it.

Nothing against Amy Grant, but this was first Jesus' grown-up Christmas list. It was a vision he once described as heaven on earth. Jesus once said you had to become like a little child in order to access and enter the kingdom of God. I think Christmas tends to bring out the child in all of us. Let's hope so.

Merry Christmas.

CHAPTER 10

"JUMP ON THE NAILS!"

There are a few friends from college I have stayed in contact with over the years. I recently met one of them for coffee when he was in the Bay Area for a conference. We had a hoot, reminiscing over our fraternity escapades and shenanigans. What always comes up is the hazing nightmare of our initiation.

It was 1976 and our initiation weekend after pledging a fraternity in college. This was back in the day when hazing was alive and well and not regulated or banned as it is today at many universities across the country. I am quite certain our fraternity would have been quickly expunged based on current anti-hazing policies.

Initiation weekend began on a Friday night, following a week of sleep deprivation, which was necessary to complete a litany of mandatory daily and nightly assignments and tasks that each pledge was given. On that Friday night after thirty minutes of verbal hazing and pushups too many to count, we were led to believe that our initiation was complete. We were taken to the large Victorian style fraternity house which stood alone on a hill—think *The Amityville Horror* house.

As we entered the house, the Actives congratulated us for successfully securing our membership into the fraternity. I thought it was odd that there was no long hazing weekend ahead as planned, but when cake and beer was ushered in, it all seemed legit. It did not take long before someone threw a piece of cake across the large dining room area where we had all congregated. It erupted into a full-on food fight with cake and beer from floor to ceiling—think *Animal House* food fight.

I was the pledge class president, and one of the Actives approached me to explain that each of us one at a time needed to go to the large pantry room in the back of the house to sign the official agreement to join the fraternity. Made sense. I was the first to go.

After being escorted to the back pantry, the door swung open and three Actives were standing around a bathtub that was full of some kind of slime. Apparently, initiation was not over. They began yelling at the top of their lungs, "Get in! Get in the tub now!!"

For the entire school semester leading up to this moment the pledges would "hash" one day a week, which meant going to the house and fixing dinner for the Actives who lived there. We prepped the food, set the table, served the meal, and supplied some form of entertainment. Afterwards we would clean up and do dishes. One frequent chore was taking the container of leftover grease from what was cooked on the large commercial grill and dumping it into a 55-gallon drum outside behind the house. Little did we know we were collecting grease that we would be submerged in and wear for nearly 40 hours, starting in that pantry room on that Friday night.

They shouted, "Get in Vleisides!!" I slowly entered the tub sliding into the grease that had been warmed up to a liquid state and with a gallon of liquid smoke added—think cauldron of witch's brew.

One by one as all the pledges were dunked and then walked throughout the house, splattering grease with the cake and beer already sloshed and smeared everywhere from the food fight. We were ordered to clean every inch of the house meticulously. The Actives watched in amusement and struck us with wooden paddles for good measure as we did. It was no easy task cleaning the house while we ourselves were dripping with grease, and the splatters each time we were whacked with the paddle.

Then came Saturday.

On Saturday afternoon we were asked, one at a time, to perform a task that seemed pointless. We were escorted into another room, told to wash our hands, given a box of 4-inch nails, and instructed to carefully clean each nail individually with cotton swabs and rubbing alcohol. There was a separate sterile box where we were told to place each disinfected nail. We had to perform this task in silence, which continued for hours without any food.

Later that evening, hungry, and exhausted, we were taken outside in the bitter winter cold, stripped naked, and an Active washed us down with a hose in order to blast off any remaining slime from the grease baptism the day before. We had all brought a coat and tie outfit to the house earlier in the week for the final initiation ceremony and told to dress in them. It seemed promising that perhaps this madness was nearing an end.

It was not.

All the pledges were collected into a separate living quarters from the house and briefed on what was coming next. Beginning with me one at a time, we were told to walk around to the front of the house and knock on the front door. As I made my way around the house, I noticed that all the indoor and outdoor lights were turned off. I knocked on the giant front door and it slowly creaked open. From there, I was given only short, terse commands. "Step inside."

Entering the dark house there were a few sparsely placed candles to provide just enough light to make your way. "Take off your socks and shoes!" came the next order. This was followed by, "Step into the pail!!" Next to a white runner on the floor there was a white metal pail, which I could smell was filled with rubbing alcohol. I stepped into it. They gave me the evil eye stare as I stood in the pail. After a couple minutes of the stare down, the next command came. "Step onto the white runner and follow it!"

I walked barefoot down the runner, which took a right turn into the now clean large dining room, which hours before had been covered in beer, cake, and grease. In front of me was a gauntlet of Actives lined up 30 men on each side facing each other with the runner on the floor between them. They were all wearing black pants, no shirts, and black hoods over their heads—think of a Church of Satan ceremony.

An Active suddenly yelled out, "Walk down the aisle!!" As I took my first step, an unintelligible mantra was being chanted in unison by the Actives. As I walked, the chant grew louder until it was thundering throughout the room and house. My heart began to pound. The white runner led to a fireplace at the other end of the room where there was a wooden chair facing away from the front of the fireplace. When I got to the front of the chair, the deafening chant abruptly ceased. A voice belted out, "Step up on the chair!!" As I did, the same voice shouted, "Look up!"

I tilted my head back and looked up to the ceiling. "Turn around!!" came the next command. Carefully maneuvering around on the chair with my head up, after I had made the turn I heard, "Look down!!" Oh my God! I looked down to see what was not there when I approached the chair moments earlier. There on the floor in front of me was a board, covered with large nails with the sharp end sticking straight up toward me. I only had a few seconds to process what I was seeing before I heard, "JUMP!! JUMP ON THE NAILS!"

What??? Are you kidding me??? Jump on the nails??? I blurted out, "NO WAY!!" It wasn't so much a "no way" in terms of a refusal to jump, as much as it was a "no way" that these guys would actually make me impale myself as a necessary rite of passage into the fraternity—think Paul Sheldon in *Misery*.

I held out momentarily, thinking that surely someone would say not to do it, it was a joke. It was not. "VLEISIDES, JUMP ON THE NAILS!!" How could I possibly do this??? I felt betrayed by these supposed "brothers." This had gone too far! As I began to become visibly angry, one of them shouted, "Trust us! Jump on the nails!" Trust them??? How??? It was an impossible situation. They were nails damnit!! Jumping on them would severely harm me, and they wanted me to "trust" them??? Another Active yelled out, "Nick, trust us! Trust the Actives! Jump on the nails!!" Then all of them together began shouting the same words, "Trust us! Jump on the nails!"

It was at this moment that they broke me. I do not know how it happened or why I did it, but I jumped. But when my feet hit the board, nothing happened. There was no piercing! The whole room erupted in laughter as I collapsed into a fetal position on the floor, an emotional wreck.

They were not nails. They were aluminum foil pieces that had been perfectly rolled and shaped into the form of nails. Looking down in the dim light you could not make out that they were anything but nails, helped along by the power of suggestion from having spent all day cleaning real nails with rubbing alcohol. From the perspective of the pledge standing on the chair there was no doubt it was those nails you were looking at! Even though the Actives got a good laugh out of this, the ritual was designed to strengthen trust between fraternity brothers, albeit a warped way of achieving it.

Sitting in Starbucks having a cup of coffee with my old college friend, we broke out howling in laughter, remembering this whole insane ordeal forty-something years ago. But then our conversation turned in to a more serious direction as he shared some of the heartaches and hardships, he had experienced over the last few years, which included a divorce, bankruptcy, and the death of his father. He divulged how this had caused a crisis of faith in his life, and that he was not sure if he believed in God any longer, or what that even meant. What does it mean to have faith or trust in God when pain and suffering have obliterated your life?

The Book of Job often comes up in discussions about God and suffering. At first glance, the story is exasperating. Job is tragically blindsided and in one instant loses everything he loves and spent his life building. He descends into the darkness of deep devastation and grief, at which time a few "friends" show up and explain to Job that his suffering is a punishment for sin, for God causes no one to suffer innocently, and they advise him to repent and seek God's mercy. We all need "friends" like that, right?

So Job, fed up with this theological nonsense that blamed him in order to defend God's character, lets the Almighty have it, calling him every name in the book and demanding an explanation. God catches wind of all this, shows up, and does not explain anything. Basically, God says to Job, "I know things you don't; trust me."

Huh? Seriously?

This takes "Jump on the nails" to a whole different level of insanity! God, who is all-good and all-powerful, stands by while your life is completely decimated, and you are supposed to trust God?

Imagine it. God escorts you down a path to a chair and tells you to stand on it. While standing on the chair you are informed that your checking and savings accounts, financial investments, and 401K no longer exist. You are then told by God that all your possessions have been destroyed. While the shock of this is sinking in, God has more horrific news. All your children have been killed. And lastly, God informs you that you have a serious and ravaging disease.

After all this, God concludes by saying, "Look, I know this seems grim. It will all work out. I promise. What I want from you is to trust me. Trust my goodness. Jump, take that leap of faith."

I cannot imagine telling a person such a thing as a first responder chaplain on the scene where tragic loss has devastated them. Last week I was dispatched to a home where a sixteen-year-old boy took his life by hanging himself from a tree in the backyard. What do I say to the mother and father? "Look, I know this is horrific. But I am here to tell you to put your trust in God. His goodness and power are deserving of your unwavering faith."

Though the tragedy and drama of Job's trial is what receives the most attention in this book, it is what happens before and after this that strikes me most. Before Job's devastation, there is a Prologue to the story in which a character identified as "the accuser" questions God's high regard for Job. The accuser contends that Job's upstanding character and deep spirituality is only because Job is blessed with great wealth, possessions, and the good fortune of having a loving family. Tinker with this, the accuser argued, and Job would be as evil, corrupt, and irreligious as anyone else. The accuser tells God he can prove this if Job had to endure hardships and tragedy. God defends Job to the accuser. In essence, God rolls the dice, believing that Job's goodness, character, and spirituality would endure.

So, Job's life is annihilated by a tragedy of epic propositions. Adding insult to injury, his "friends" tell Job that the cause of the trial is God's punishment for his sins. In the heat of the moment, Job has a meltdown and blows up at God, which is understandable, given the circumstances. God shows up and though he does not give any explanation for the cause of Job's suffering, he instead invites and challenges Job to consider the possibility that there is something afoot in the world that is greater than what he is seeing and experiencing in the moment of his heartache, grief, anger, and despair.

We are told in the story that after all of this, Job reaffirms his faith and trust. Faith and trust in what? Faith and trust in a process that is the heart and the very essence of life itself, a quality or intention that imbues the very nature of reality. I think of that process, essence, intention as God.

In the Epilogue of the story, we discover that Job finds healing, recovery, and restoration. He gets back on his feet financially and rebuilds his life. His brothers and sisters surrounded him with love and support. He and his wife gave birth to several sons and daughters.

There is a lot we do not understand about how God relates to suffering. But there is something to learn from Job about how we relate to suffering. When our lives are struck down by hardship, loss, and tragedy, there will unfortunately be no shortage of people who will say stupid things, trying to explain it. Some of these people will even be good-intentioned people trying to comfort us.

In times of heartache and suffering, it is normal, expected, and even necessary to feel the full range of volatile emotions, including sorrow, grief, anger, and despair. It is okay to feel what you feel. We laugh, cry, dance, feel ecstasy, even feel despair. It is how we know the world. It is how we live inside of our hearts and not dissociated from them.

Built into the very process and essence of life itself is the possibility and potential of getting through our hardships, recovering from its impact, integrating our heartaches and losses into our lives, being deepened and transformed by the process, find new life after it, and becoming human beings of greater empathy and compassion for others in their suffering.

There will be times in life when we lose trust and faith in God. But consider the possibility that God never loses trust and faith in you. God's estimation and regard for you is never diminished. God is no fool, he will always roll the dice, believing in you.

CHAPTER 11

THE DEFINITION OF YOU

There will be blood. In this case, there was so much of it that the referee decided to end the soccer game. No, it was not a hooligan riot in a World Cup qualifying match, it was my 14-year-old daughter's youth soccer scrimmage. Noelle's feet got tangled up with an opposing player and tumbled to the ground, where she received one nasty soccer cleat kick to the face, which opened a large laceration on her forehead. As Murphy's Law (and afternoon rush hour in San Francisco) goes, Heidi and I were stuck in traffic and late to the scrimmage, when the coach called to inform us what had happened. She wrapped a 4-inch gauze bandage around her head and called an ambulance. Noelle was being transported to San Francisco General Hospital, which was our next exit. We arrived before the ambulance did.

We were concerned about the possibility that she had suffered a concussion or serious brain injury. When the ER doctor removed the bandage from her head, all of us got a good look at the laceration for the first time. I am sure Noelle caught the distraught expressions on everyone's faces, as the deep cut stretched from her nose to her hairline, exposing a part of her skull. Noelle had a slight concussion but no further head injury. She received a nice long row of stitches from the plastic surgeon on duty, and her soccer season was over. There were a few more doctor visits, but eventually she healed from her injury and all was well. The ordeal left a noticeable scar on her forehead, which you can still see today.

We were worried about how this facial scar would affect Noelle's feelings about herself, being the 14-year-old girl that she was. At her age, physical appearance was everything, and there was no disentangling body image from self-esteem. As it turns out, Noelle accepted her scar like it was a badge of honor. There was an endearing aspect to her scar that to me made her more beautiful. Noelle was not defeated by this traumatic event, even though it left a permanent memento on her forehead.

I have learned in life that it is the scars you do not see that are not so easy to recover from. Over the course of more than two decades as a first responder chaplain, I have encountered some of the most horrific and heartbreaking human tragedies. In every traumatic scenario, there always comes that discomforting moment when it is time for me to leave a scene. Driving away, I am aware that the harrowing events in my rearview mirror will leave a permanent emotional scar upon the lives of those impacted by them.

A mother who finds her dead son hanging from a rope in the garage; a father informed by police at his front door that his teenage daughter was killed by a drunk driver; a community in grief and shock from a mass school shooting; the family left behind after their father suffers a massive heart attack at dinner and dies; a young woman who has been the victim of rape—these are tragedies you never really "recover" from. To refer to them as "scars" is an understatement, it is more like an amputation.

I have been told by amputees that they often feel phantom pains. The limb they lost still announces its presence through pain. Likewise, for those who have endured irreversible loss such as the death of a loved one, their absence is felt in emotional pain. There are reminders of their loss everywhere. Just as the amputee is forced to accept and adjust to a new set of life circumstances, so does the person who suffers catastrophic loss. Whereas the amputee wakes up each day without a leg or arm, the other wakes up without a son or daughter, or mother or father, husband, or wife.

Loss often creates a crisis of identity. We tend to derive our strongest sense of self from the roles we play and our most cherished relationships as a parent, spouse, and as adult children. When these roles and relationships are changed or lost, we find ourselves in identity vertigo. One of the most devastating losses I learned about as a first responder chaplain was a man who was stripped of everything in an instant when a tragic car accident claimed three generations of his family: his mother, his wife, and his young daughter. One of the things he expressed during his grieving process was, "I don't know who I am anymore."

Tragedy and loss force us to grapple with life's biggest existential questions about the meaning of our lives, and our most fundamental sense of identity. Who are we after tragedy rips a loved one from our lives, or we forfeit our health to serious injury, disease or illness? Who are we after the loss of a job or career, financial collapse, or the relinquishment of a dream? When we painfully lose a marriage through divorce, or deprived of relationship with our children through separation or estrangement, who are we then? Who are we after our mental, emotional, physical, or sexual wholeness and wellbeing has been stolen from us through victimization and abuse?

For most people, our sense of self is built on a fragile foundation. Our roles and relationships, health and vigor, career and security, and success and prosperity do not have an absolute, guaranteed, or stable nature to them. They are characterized by impermanence, change, and unpredictability. They often depend on factors outside our control. Most of us can keep the illusion of permanence, security, and control going until tragedy and loss strikes. Our grief, heartache, suffering, and anguish forces us to swallow the bitter pill of reality.

Therefore, people become angry with God when tragedy befalls them. In their mind, this was not supposed to happen. The death of their son or daughter was not supposed to happen. A terminal illness diagnosis does not lineup with "God's perfect plan." Losing everything and filing bankruptcy was not supposed to happen. Betrayal and divorce are not something that one should expect as a devoted Christian.

Last week a wife took her 54 year old husband to the Emergency Room after complaining all day about a feeling of indigestion. At the ER they discovered he was having heart problems. They rushed him to the Cath Lab to insert a stint and he died during the process. His young adult son and daughter showed up. I met them in a small, dank hospital room where they sat stunned, lost, inconsolable and devastated. "How could you, God?!"

Debilitating depression is not supposed to affect a person of faith. God was not supposed to let any of this happen. If God cannot prevent or stop this from occurring, what good is he? If God is "all-good and all-powerful," why does this happen? What exactly does God offer me that I can take refuge in?

One of the biggest misconceptions about God and faith, is that if we do our part (faith and obedience), God is obligated to do his part (protect and prosper us). Do good things, good things happen—do bad things, bad things happen. This is the Santa Claus version of God in which he sees who has been "naughty or nice" and rewards them accordingly.

Let us ponder this idea.

First off, the notion of pleasing or obeying God in order to gain favorable life circumstances as "God's blessing" is false. The world is characterized by impermanence and was never intended to be the source of true peace, happiness, contentment, and well-being. There is no measure of pleasing or obeying God that is ever going to change the transitory nature of the world. Thoughts, feelings, finances, health, job, relationships, situations, conditions, circumstances, possessions, abilities, etc. are all characterized by impermanence and subject to change. And none of these things are entirely within our control.

As a rule of thumb, responding to life situations as they require with wisdom and skill will yield a better result than responding out of ignorance and incompetence. Likewise, if we sow seeds of love, generosity, and compassion in our lives we are likely to reap a quality of life that is more enriching than if we sow seeds of hatred, selfishness, and bitterness.

But the idea that obedience, faithfulness, and spiritual maturity should result in God blessing our lives with favorable circumstances and protecting us from hardship and tragedy, is unreal. If this were true, God really missed the boat when it came to Jesus, who experienced levels of physical, mental, emotional, and psychological suffering that few people ever have or will.

The reason why people are so caught up in currying favor with God is that they wrongly assume that the trick to happiness is to coax God into "blessing" our lives by meddling in our circumstances to give us what we want and prevent what we don't. But God is not going to cooperate with that strategy or formula. Why? Because God does not care or is malevolent? No. It is because your circumstances are irrelevant to having true peace, well-being, and happiness. We seek the blessings, not the Blessor.

Even if God gave you everything you wanted and prevented everything you did not, you will not have true peace and happiness. In fact, all that would happen is that you would be requesting more and more from God. Why? Because the transitory nature of everything in the world means that you can never derive an absolute, ultimate, or perpetual satisfaction and contentment from it.

The entire premise that you as a human being down here on earth must appease and appeal to a God in the heavens in order for said God to pull strings and bless you with favorable circumstances to be happy, is flawed from start to finish. It assumes there is a "you" and there is a separate "God" out there somewhere in the space.

The Bible says that God is spirit. In other words, God is not an entity or object found in some specific place in the universe. God is infinite, timeless, clear, radiant, limitless, complete, untroubled, consistent essence. The Apostle Paul described this vast essence and nature of God in his Epistle to the Romans, by saying, "For from God and through God and to God are all things."

The second "God is…" statement in the Bible is, "God is love." God being "spirit" or "essence" does not mean that God is some impersonal, detached, abstract energy vibrating in space. The nature or essence of God has a personal component to it, which we access through the experiences of love, compassion, and belonging. There is the seen, and there is the unseen.

Though we human beings suffer a crisis of identity when our lives are turned upside down by loss and tragedy, there is never a moment when our most fundamental well-being is ever threatened or diminished. The first thing we are told about ourselves in the Book of Genesis is that we are made in the image of God. In other words, that vast, infinite, radiant, complete, whole, serene, undisturbed image, essence, or nature of God is the primordial, underlying, and fundamental essence of who you and I are.

Our true nature is a manifestation of the essence and nature of God, perpetually abiding in peace, love, well-being, wholeness, harmony, and serenity. Who we yearn to become in the world, we already are at the deepest level. What we seek God for in our obedience, faithfulness, and devotion, we already have in our true nature because you are never separated from God and because you are joined to God by sharing in his essence and nature, you are never separated from peace, love, well-being, wholeness, harmony, and serenity.

People seek and search for God every day, thinking God is out there somewhere. People chase love, peace, happiness, well-being, freedom, and wholeness every day because they think they do not have them. People experience a crisis of identity because they imagine they do not have a whole and stable self. But none of this is true. You do have these. You are not separated from them. They are not out there somewhere to hunt down. That cannot be taken from us. We may lose our health, financial security, and even those we love, but we will never lose or be separated from our true nature.

At the deepest level of who you are, there is no drama of chasing happiness. Your true self is not chasing anything. There is only a deep-rooted awareness that all is well. There is no fear or disturbance. There is only acceptance and contentment. At the deepest level you are one with God. In that place you cannot disentangle yourself and God because they are one. If you look for God, you will find yourself. If you look for yourself, you will find God. God does not lack anything. You do not lack anything. God is not disturbed. You are not disturbed. God is peace and well-being. You are peace and well-being.

You go to church to find God but any God you find in church you bring in with you. You consume book after book in search of truth that is already woven into the essence of who you are. You practice spiritual disciplines in the hopes of attaining an inner peace that you have never lost. There is nothing to gain because there is nothing missing. It is not entering a new reality because there is only one reality, and you have never left it.

What defines you? Your physical health? Your financial wellbeing? The roles and relationships you have in life? Your success and achievements? Your possessions? Your status and reputation? The loved ones you have built your life around? Yes, it is true that our lives consist of all those realities. That is not a problem. It is only a problem if we presume that these are permanent and absolute. We can lose our health, career, finances, possessions, status, relationships, and even lose the people we most love but you will never lose connection to the true source of love, happiness, peace, contentment, serenity, strength, wisdom, and compassion.

When tragedy and loss strike us, who we are in relative terms to the people, places, and circumstances of our lives are thrown into chaos and our relative identity is destabilized. We say things like, "I don't know who I am anymore." We feel heartache, grief, despair, and loss. We are scarred. Our feelings of volatility in those moments are normal and part of what it means to be human.

Emily Dickinson wrote,

"Hope is the thing with feathers
That perches in the soul
And sings the tune without the words
And never stops at all."

This hope is the spirit and essence of God, which constitutes your true nature. It is that thing with feathers, perched in your soul and never stops singing the tune of the truth of who you are.

I once responded to a call involving a Native American man. His father who lived with him had suffered an aortic aneurysm and died, despite the efforts of first responders to save him. While at the man's home I noticed feathers displayed in several places. Feathers have long been associated with Native American culture especially eagle feathers, but I have never quite understood why. I asked him about it, and he explained that the feather is a symbol of the Great Spirit from whom all strength and power flows.

God is spirit. We all sense it. Whether it is Emily Dickenson, Sitting Bull, or Moses, they all attested to a vast spirit that fills the universe. But not only that, it sits perched in our soul and sings hope, strength, power, and peace to us... and never stops at all.

CHAPTER 12

PLAN B

It was a majestic drive up the narrow winding road that overlooked Oak River Canyon. Scents of oak and cedar wafted through the pure clean air beneath a cloudless, sapphire blue sky. Unfortunately, this was not a Sunday scenic drive or outdoors adventure. At the end of this winding road was the scene where a 911 call was made. The narrow road turned into a driveway, and the distressing situation came into full view. A car was wedged between two oak trees, which for the time being were preventing it from free falling into the canyon below. A man was trapped inside the vehicle.

As I approached closer, the man's distraught wife ran up to my car in the driveway screaming, "Help him! Please help him!" Rarely am I ever the first to arrive on scene but because I happened to be only a few minutes from the location when I received the dispatch call, my arrival was swift. The woman frantically explained what had happened.

Her husband had parked their car facing down the driveway on the descending slope toward the canyon. When he exited the vehicle and started to walk away, the car slowly began rolling down and off the driveway. To rescue the car from plunging into the abyss of the canyon below, he chased it down and opened the door of the moving car to jump into the driver's seat. As he did this, the vehicle rolled off the driveway and began plummeting down the cliff. It was miraculously caught by two oak trees, leaving the vehicle wedged between the two oaks with the man partially hanging out of the door.

Approaching the vehicle, I saw his head sticking out between the top of the door jam and the roof of the car, with blood streaming down the window. I assumed the man was dead. Surveying the situation, I made out a faint moaning and shouted down to the voice below. He cried out, "I need help! Somebody help me!" I assured him that help was coming and focused on calming the man down, which also required calming his wife down in her own understandable but counterproductive hysterics.

It was a tense situation. I did not know how long these oak trees would hold the car in place until they gave to or snapped. I radioed an assessment to the crews on the way, and a heavy rescue vehicle was dispatched to the scene. A heavy rescue vehicle is a specialty emergency bus, which holds rescue apparatus such as the Jaws of Life, crane, hi-lift jacks, and cutting torches.

When emergency teams arrived, it was quickly determined that the plan of action was to first secure the car to prevent it from dislodging from the trees and plunging to the bottom of the canyon, which would mean certain death. Once this was done, the plan was to cut down the oak trees so the vehicle and the man could more easily be pulled back up to solid ground.

Through skilled maneuvering, the crane was used to lock metal chains and lifting hooks around the vehicle. Then, search and rescue specialists rappelled down the cliff to blow-torch the car door off in order to assess the man's condition. What they quickly discovered was alarmingly fortunate. The man's head and neck was protruding out the top of the door frame, while his ankle had been caught in the door below. It was the man's ankle wedged in the door at the bottom, which had prevented the door from severing off the man's head.

136

It was difficult to determine what internal injuries he might have suffered, but paramedics suspected from what they saw and their interactions with the man, that he likely had avulsion wounds, broken ribs and leg, and some form of concussion or brain injury.

The paramedics explained to the man that the plan was to cut the oak trees in order to pull him and his vehicle back up to the driveway. The rescue team had already retrieved their chainsaws and were moving into position to saw the trees.

Suddenly, the man belted out, "NO!" Everyone stopped to see what had happened. Any number of things can quickly go wrong in a rescue operation like this. Time is of the essence, when the full extent of a victim's injuries has not yet been determined.

To everyone's astonishment, the man continued, "No! Not my oaks. Don't cut my oak trees. Please." Everyone looked at each other, perplexed. Huh? Are you kidding!? This guy is in a vehicle suspended between two trees, which could become dislodged sending him and his car into a freefall to the bottom of the canyon resulting in certain death. Initial assessments were that he had serious injuries. And he wanted to save the trees?

The man was adamant and pleaded with the crew not to cut the trees down. He was quite distressed about it, making matters worse and jeopardizing the whole operation. In less than a minute, Plan B was created and sprang into action. With the car door already removed, a rescue stretcher was lowered and the man was carefully removed from the vehicle, strapped to the stretcher, and pulleyed up to solid ground. Once the okay was given, the rescue team got out the hydraulic spreaders and cutters and proceeded to tear his car apart to get it out. The good news was that the man did not have life-threatening injuries. He managed to escape the ordeal with third-degree abrasions, mild concussion, bruised ribs, and a broken ankle.

As the ambulance howled off to the nearby hospital, the rest of us began packing up equipment, loading vehicles, and other post-rescue logistics. When everything was ready to go, the rescue team captain thanked and praised everyone for the success of the effort, and then with a relieved but slightly disbelieving look on his face said, "Thank god for Plan B!" We all laughed, and roared, "Here, here! Plan B!" as if we were raising our glasses for a celebratory toast.

Later that evening at home Heidi asked me how things had gone on my chaplain call. I told her it was great—that we had rescued a man and two oak trees. She looked perplexed. I explained the entire ordeal and rescue operation, including Plan B and saving the trees. Heidi was amused and then she said, "Well, yeah, that's pretty much life isn't it, Plan B."

Heidi's words hung around in my head and heart for the next couple of days: Life is Plan B.

She is right. We all have a Plan A, which is the way we want life to be and how we want our lives to go. We have our goals and aspirations, hopes and dreams, intentions and desires, and a picture in our mind of a satisfying, fulfilling, successful, great life. We not only have a big-picture Plan A, we also have a Plan A for every day. The daily Plan A is the way we want to move through our day, effortlessly, productively, contentedly, untroubled, and free of all stress, difficult, or hardship. It includes blue skies, agreeable children, perfect cup of coffee, no traffic, profitable endeavors, guilt-free chocolate cake, relaxing evening, and sound sleep.

The only thing about Plan A is that it hardly ever happens. Life just won't cooperate. Unrealized dreams, broken relationships, financial pressures, difficult people, and sleepless nights get in the way. We discover there is no such thing as guilt-free chocolate cake. Life is rarely Plan A. Even if everything lines up perfectly for some stretch of time, it never stays that way. Life lacks permanence, things are always changing, and many variables that impact our lives are outside our control.

Every chaplain call I respond to is a Plan B scenario. No one expects or is truly prepared for tragedy and catastrophic loss. Think about the chaplain scenarios I have already described so far in this book. Not one person would have wanted these heartbreaking catastrophes or devastating hardships to happen. Life does not go as planned, and is often jolted into a direction we would not have chosen.

Despite the power we ascribe to God, even the Almighty had to go with Plan B. The Garden of Eden was Plan A, where everything was characterized by perfect peace, joy, harmony, and serenity. You know the story; it did not last too long. In the Garden of Gethsemane, Jesus indicated that dying a brutal death on a cross was not his Plan A and inquired to God if another scenario was possible. Saint Paul, who wrote most of the New Testament, was constantly afflicted by trials and tribulations, including beatings, torture, starvation, shipwrecks, stoning, isolation, depression, and imprisonment. Certainly not what he was hoping for.

Point to any person throughout all of history who we remember and honor as having embodied heroic courage, extraordinary achievement, selfless service, highest virtue, or magnificent creativity, and you will see that a lot of Plan B was happening. In fact, I cannot think of one human being ever who perfectly pulled off Plan A. Every human life involves Plan B, and typically Plan C, D, E, and F.

I looked up the definition of Plan B, and it states that it is "...an action or set of actions for doing or achieving something that can be used if the preferred method fails." Hmmm. According to the definition, Plan B has to do with method.

All human beings want to be happy. Right? No sane person wants to be miserable, joyless, tormented, empty, impoverished, and suffering. But what if the problem is not that we cannot have happiness, peace, meaning, fulfillment, equanimity, and contentment, but that our preferred method of acquiring it is the problem?

Plan A is based upon two faulty premises. The first false premise is that if I get what I want then I will be happy. Closely related is the second faulty premise, if I can avoid what I do not want I will be happy.

We all tend to think that if we had a certain "thing" in our lives that we would find happiness. That "thing" could range from career success, perfect relationship, financial independence, bigger home, thinner waistline, or popularity. Whatever that "thing" is for you or me, we tend to think that if we had it, we would be happy.

I am not saying it is "wrong" to want those things. Everyone would agree that it would be beneficial to have meaningful relationships, good health, accomplished goals, and the simple enjoyments and pleasures of life. What I am questioning is the part that says if we have or acquire these things that this will make us happy.

The reason why I am questioning this is because any "thing" we would depend upon for our happiness, is characterized by that impermanence and change I alluded to earlier. Virtually all the things we want in life depend upon numerous variables outside our control. Successful relationships are not based solely on what you do, your income and expenses are often affected by unforeseen circumstances, the composition and shape of your body is impacted by genes, age, and medical conditions. Virtually everything in the world has a relative existence. Though things appear to be separate and absolute unto themselves, they actually exist in interdependence with everything else. What this means is that all these things we depend upon for our happiness are not truly stable, dependable, or reliable.

This is why we are so disappointed and disheartened when the things we rely upon for happiness change, fade, or perish. At some level we were counting on them to have a rocklike and stable nature to them, which they do not have.

Neither is it possible to avoid all the things we do not want. Even if we could somehow always make perfect choices and take perfect actions to avoid hardship, difficulty, loss, and tragedy, we could not prevent them entirely because we do not have control over all the factors that could cause them.

If Plan A is based upon getting what you want and avoiding what you do not, Plan A will never work. It is fundamentally flawed and doomed. The method that Plan A relies upon is not capable of producing the outcome we want.

But what if there was another way? What if there was a different plan that is based upon a stable, dependable, trustworthy and true source of peace, happiness, equanimity, and contentment? And what if that source is available and accessible to you right now, and every moment of your life? What if this method for happiness did not rely upon variables outside your control or things that have an unreliable and unstable nature to them? What if this plan is the perfect plan and the only one that can ever work?

Consider the possibility that your happiness is not contingent upon any "thing" out there in the world to be gained, achieved, earned or avoided.

The very first thing we are told about ourselves in the Bible is that our fundamental nature is a manifestation of the life, essence, and image of God. God is our ground of being. This means that at the most fundamental level of who you are, you share in the perfect peace, serenity, love, wisdom, strength, wisdom and wholeness that is God. Your true nature is characterized by composure, joy, compassion, and clarity.

Becoming more familiar and attuned to this life and nature within us is the only reliable path of happiness. It allows us to approach life from a place of inner equanimity and contentment. We are able to appreciate life as it unfolds, without projecting our expectations and demands that it be what we want it to be to make us happy. We are able to absorb our tragedies, hardships, and losses into the strength, wisdom, and wholeness within us.

This plan involves a liberating shift of focus and mindset in life from "how can I get things to make me happy" to "how can I become more familiar with and attuned to my true nature." As it stands now for most people, 95%–100% of our time, energy, focus is devoted to the former, while 0%–5% is devoted to the latter. What that means is that most of us have never even tried the only plan that truly works for having true happiness.

G.K. Chesterton pointed out that the reason Christianity seems to fail people is not because it has been tried and found wanting, but because it has been left untried. Contrary to popular belief, Christianity is not going to church, checking the boxes, being good or at least not caught, and going to heaven when you die. Christianity is fundamentally harmonizing our lives with the presence of God that is within us and is us. Our innermost self, true nature, and ground of being is the absolute and complete joy, peace, security, abundance, happiness, and wellbeing we long for. No "thing" in the world can produce or deliver this, it can only be found inside ourselves where God meets us.

Many people become disillusioned with God because they were expecting him to operate on the level of Plan A. Why would God participate in a method that does not work and only leads to suffering? Instead, God provided Plan B—the perfect plan, the only plan that will ever work.

A couple of days after our rescue operation I was visiting a friend in the hospital who had back surgery. I discovered that the man rescued from the dangling vehicle was also there recovering from his injuries. I stopped by his room to see how he was doing. In addition to his fractured ribs and concussion, he had shattered his right tibia, fibula, and talus, which required surgery. All things considered; he was recovering well.

As we chatted, I brought up those two oak trees. Turns out that the oak tree belongs to the Quercus genus tree species—there are up to 800 species all over the world, especially in the Northern hemisphere where they are native. It is a tree that can live more than 1000 years. Some are able to reach 70 feet in height, 135 feet in length, and 9 feet wide.

Numerous animals subsist on the acorns and leaves dropped by oak trees. Oak wood is well known for being hardy and strong. Oak makes solid furniture, ships, floors, and Yamaha drums are even made out of oak trees! The Greeks believed oaks to be a sacred tree of Zeus, the king of the gods. The oak tree is considered a cosmic storehouse of wisdom embodied in its towering strength. Oak trees are often associated with honor, nobility, and wisdom, and are a powerful life-affirming symbol. I learned all that and more.

George Bernard Shaw wrote, "Think of the fierce energy concentrated in an acorn! You bury it in the ground, and it explodes into an oak!"

I guess the captain was right, "Thank God for Plan B!"

CHAPTER 13

RULE BREAKER

Christianity is all about keeping the rules, and Jesus was all about breaking them.

Is it me or is there something off about that?

This came into full focus for me while attending an Easter church service in a little town tucked away in the Sierra Mountains of Northern California.

For twenty-five years my in-laws owned a little cabin in Arnold, California. Arnold is an area less than 15 square miles, with a population under 4,000. The quaint town is in Stanislaus National Forest, 900,000 acres stretched across four counties in the Sierra Nevada. It is one of the oldest national forests, which sits next to the northwestern part of Yosemite National Park.

For many years, Heidi and I and the kids would take summer trips to visit my in-laws at their cabin. We have many fond family memories of enjoying the great outdoors—fishing, dirt biking, four wheeling, hiking, and skiing. Sadly, my in-laws eventually sold their place, but we still occasionally find our way to Arnold for a family getaway.

Over the years we became friends with other families who lived in or frequented Arnold. Recently, one of those families offered for us to stay at their cabin while they were out of the country. The kids are older now, but two of the three were able to go with us. Our stay included being there over the Easter weekend. The plan was to do some skiing. A lot of snow had fallen in the Sierra since January and the slopes were perfect for an alpine adventure.

My friend's place was just around the corner from my in-laws' old cabin. The next morning after we arrived, I took a walk by the cabin, which was a nostalgic trip down memory lane. It amazed me how everything looked exactly the same. Rounding the curve as I continued walking through this wooded hamlet of homey cabins, I noticed up the road a man and woman conversing in the street. They looked to be about in their 70's, and it appeared the man was out walking his dog and stopped for a neighborly chat with the woman in front of her cottage.

As I walked past them the man greeted me to which I politely obliged and returned the sentiment. Then he stepped toward me and stuck out his hand introducing himself with a firm handshake. I introduced myself to both, and they asked if I was visiting Arnold. This led to a conversation about my in-law's cabin around the corner, and our family visiting the area for a few days by invitation from a friend. Being Easter weekend, the man inquired if we would be attending church, and invites us to go to the Easter service at his church in Arnold.

There are several churches in and around Arnold—a Catholic church, Episcopal church, and a few non-denominational and evangelical churches. I accepted the man's invitation to his place of worship, and our family attended their Easter Sunday service. I had gone to this church a couple times over the years during our trips to visit Heidi's parents.

Driving up the gravel entrance, lined with cedar and pine trees, we parked in front of this serene wood and stone church. A large group of folks from the earlier service were gathered out front enjoying coffee, donuts, and friendly chit-chat. I must admit it was a bit awkward when our family piled out of our Ford F250 Super Duty long bed truck and strolled past this crowd of gathered church members without so much as a glance from anyone and walked into the front of the church.

We were handed a paper bulletin with the order of service and some announcements by a little girl in a solid yellow Easter dress who politely but shyly greeted us by saying, "Welcome. Happy Easter!" The sanctuary of this little old church could hold about 200 people, and we managed to find a row we could all squeeze into. I am sure we stuck out as visitors. We are not exactly the family that just blends in—our daughter is 5'11" and our son 6'1"—but still, no one spoke a word to us or even looked our way.

The service was somewhat traditional but had a contemporary style worship band. We sang a few conventional Easter hymns and then a few upbeat praise songs. There are a few subjects you might expect to hear in an Easter Sunday sermon, most notably about the risen Christ, resurrection hope, defeating death, and new life.

Not this Easter sermon.

This one was titled, "The Rule-Breaker in the Mirror."

Do not ask me how it is possible to turn the triumphant, celebratory, vitalizing, and hope-inspiring tone of Resurrection Sunday into a sermon about how each of us broke God's one and only original rule, making us all guilty sinners with the blood of Jesus on our hands, and undeserving of the eternal life he achieved by subjecting himself to the wrath of God, which we had coming.

Happy Easter!

The pastor admitted at the start of the sermon that a message on sin was not usually what someone would expect to hear on Easter. But since Easter Sunday is the most heavily attended church service of the year, he explained that he felt a divine duty to preach the "true gospel" and how this was a fitting way to honor the death and resurrection of Jesus.

So, a sermon on sin, it was.

Here is the gist. God made a perfect paradise for Adam and Eve to enjoy eternal fellowship with God. All they had to do was keep one rule, not to partake of the fruit of the forbidden tree. Adam and Eve brazenly and defiantly broke God's only rule. This means that each of us as Adam and Eve's offspring are born as rulebreakers with a sinful and defiant nature toward God. The only way for God to remedy this problem was to require the death of his son on the cross. Now God's only rule is to repent and accept Jesus as your Lord and Savior. Most people refuse to follow this one rule as well. While there are some who want Jesus to be their Savior, they are not willing to follow him as Lord.

Try as you may, you really cannot get this out of the Bible exactly that way.

It has always been curious to me that the cornerstone of this version of "the gospel" is the idea that humankind is born with "original sin." The Bible tells the story of humankind's relationship with God. The story begins in the Book of Genesis when God creates the world and humankind and declares all of it to be good. Yes, that is right—not bad but *good!* You cannot undo what God did. Regardless of what a person does with their God-given nature, they cannot undo it. God's being is the ground of your being, which means at the most fundamental level your true nature is clean, clear, pure, complete, and good.

Contrary to widely held belief, the "gospel" is *not*:

- a sin-management system

- behavior-modification program

- a ticket punched for heaven

- doctrinal litmus test

- eternal fire insurance

- checklist of religious do's and don'ts

- a cure for your badness

- an appeasement of an angry God

- bargaining chip for God's blessing

The doctrine of "original sin" is exactly that—a doctrine—developed by the early Church fathers such as Irenaeus and Augustine in the 2nd century. It asserts that all human beings are born with a sin nature as a result of Adam and Eve's rebellion against God in Eden. According to the doctrine, humanity shares in Adam and Eve's sin because it is transmitted genetically. It is in our DNA. This idea is not unique to Christianity.

The issue needing resolution regarding "original sin" was: How did evil enter the world if God is good? Answer: Adam and Eve's disobedience.

The doctrine of original sin upholds the following:

1. That the Bible's creation story is meant to be taken literally—that there was an actual Adam and Eve who were the first human beings, and that the family tree of all humankind is traced back to them.

2. That Adam and Eve's act of disobedience and rebellion of God resulted in a sinful condition that can be propagated through human conception and birth. Hence the doctrine of the virgin birth—the belief that Mary was *not* impregnated through the sperm of Joseph, which would have

been contaminated by the sinful condition, but impregnated directly by God himself.

The Bible itself seems to be contradictory when it comes to the matter of original sin, and there is no consistent or coherent message about it. The Apostle Paul wrote that "all have sinned and fall short of the glory of God," and yet Jesus himself said, "blessed are the pure in heart," implying that one's innermost being is untainted. It is also interesting to note that the Apostle Paul in all of his letters always refers to his readers in the salutation as "saints," never "sinners."

As mentioned, in the Genesis creation story prior to the fall of Adam and Eve, God's original pronouncement upon all creation, including the human person, is that they are "good" and a manifestation of the very image or essence of God. Regardless of our thoughts, actions, and behaviors in any given moment, there is a spark of divinity in all of us. All of us. Always.

So, the question is, why have we allowed the doctrine of original sin to become so central to Christianity? I am not saying there is no use for doctrine that is helpful but for heaven's sake, do we have to accept every doctrine at face value when it is very possible it is not correct and possibly leads us away from the truth about God? Florence Nightingale wrote, "What are now called "essential doctrines" of the Christian religion, Christ does not even mention." It would be impossible to imagine anything more un-Christlike than theology developed by mere man uninspired by God. Christ probably couldn't have understood it.

People once believed the world was flat and the earth was the center of the universe, but once they were given more accurate information, they eventually adopted the new view. And yet, people hold onto religious beliefs despite their absurdity and the absence of evidence.

Religious truth is often held to a different standard. It gets a pass in terms of how we typically determine the truth of a proposition.

When a religious belief appears unfounded or illogical, we often hear the phrase, "God's ways are not our ways." It is considered the height of arrogance to think one can understand the ways of God with the human mind. After all, God is "omniscient" or all-knowing. Who are we to question? Right?

Insert the carrot and the stick. Let us say you believe there is a God who rewards and punishes people, and that your eternal future of heaven or hell are hanging in the balance. If the authoritative people (clergy, early church fathers, Bible scholars) impart a set of beliefs you are expected to uphold to remain in good standing with God, then you could be persuaded to accept any number of unnecessary or even absurd things. The alternative would be to question them, jeopardizing your standing with the Almighty or being labeled a heretic. So, could it be that the short answer to why people who should know better believe nonsensical religious ideas is fear?

In seminary I took a class on the book of Genesis. The traditional interpretation of the story commonly referred to as "the Fall," has been difficult to accept. In conservative Christian tradition and doctrine the story is believed to be a literal historical event. But the liberal view is that the story is meant to be figurative containing several themes. No matter, the themes are what is worth considering most.

In my view, Eve is the daring and courageous one. God said do not eat from the tree of the knowledge of good and evil.

Let us digress momentarily to consider the context here.

Just hang with me here as I state what is a struggle to believe for many. The picture Genesis presents of God is one who is complicated, seemingly contradictory, capricious, and at times, capable of evil, or at least the creator or manipulator of evil. Why would God put the Tree of the Knowledge of Good and Evil in the Garden, knowing full well that Adam and Eve would do the very thing he told them not to? Put a bunch of people in a room with two windows and say to them, whatever you do just do not look through the window on the right. What do you think they will all do? They will do exactly that.

Why would God risk the well-being of his entire created order by telling Adam and Eve not to do something he knew they would? The way the story is framed, regardless of the role of the serpent, one could argue that God is ultimately responsible and the one to blame for "the Fall." If we are not afraid to admit it, this dilemma of how to comprehend God is real for many.

In my mind, Eve is the first rule-breaker. Eleanor Roosevelt wrote, "Well-behaved women seldom make history." Enter Eve. God said do not eat from the tree of the knowledge of good and evil. Yet, we all know that the world often makes its greatest advances by disobedient people who break the rules. Think Galileo, Gandhi, Martin Luther King, Jr., Nelson Mandela, Susan B. Anthony, Malala Yousafzai. Martin Luther King, Jr. wrote, "Disobedience is the true foundation of liberty." Henry David Thoreau wrote, "You can best serve civilization by being against what usually passes for it."

God tells Adam and Eve not to eat the fruit, but they never promise not to. In their minds, they surely were not consciously against God. They were curiously tempted. Should they have been obedient? Let us think about it. How obedient do you want your children to be? You want them to be obedient enough so that they do not get hurt, but disobedient enough so that they go out in the world and live authentically, courageously, autonomously, and freely.

On one level, Eve's decision made complete sense. According to the text, Eve chose to eat the fruit from the forbidden tree because:

1. it was necessary for sustenance—it was "good for food"

2. it resonated with her aesthetic sensibilities—it was "pleasing to the eye"

3. it would contribute to her growth and maturity—"desirable for gaining wisdom

If I came to you and said, "I want to offer you something—it is necessary to live, pleasing and satisfying, and will transform your entire way of being in the world. Are you interested?" My guess is that you would say, "Yes!" In addition to all that, Eve did not selfishly claim it all for herself. She shared the fruit with her partner, Adam.

Meanwhile, notice that even though Adam did not have the moxie to break the rules and risk taking the fruit himself, he had no problem gladly accepting it from Eve. And yet, Adam blames both God and Eve for the whole ordeal. Adam says, "The woman YOU PUT HERE with me—SHE gave me some fruit from the tree..." Adam plays the victim card and throws his partner under the bus to save himself, which is quite unbecoming and disgracing.

Eve also played the blame-game by telling God, "the devil (serpent) made me do it." She has a point though; that serpent was quite crafty. Where did he come from anyway?

This is the only thing I wish Eve had done differently. I would have preferred her being more forthcoming with God and say something like:

"Okay, God. Here is the deal. Yes, I did it. I know you said not to eat from that tree. You also gave me a curious brain to use and I did. I never promised I would not. I was feeling it. So, I went for it. I put on my big-girl panties and ate the fruit. I did not mean any disrespect to you. I'm not against you. I was doing me. Actions have consequences. I get that now. Lesson learned."

Taking this account metaphorically, I think the idea was to construct a story that sets up the complexities of properly executing our freedom and agency in the world. God's edict not to eat from the tree of the knowledge of good and evil is depicted as a safeguard to protect Adam and Eve from shouldering too heavy a burden of understanding the world and life in its most transparent terms. In other words, to know the world, particularly in its most frightening potentialities and possibilities, in which only God could see. After eating the fruit, we are told their eyes were opened, which means God initially had put blinders on them, so they were not capable of seeing the whole deal.

The knowledge of good and evil can be seen in the story in two ways. On the one hand, you might say that ignorance is bliss. Not having this knowledge was a feature of the paradise and harmony that was depicted prior to eating the forbidden fruit/knowledge. On the other hand, Eve saw that eating the fruit would be "gaining wisdom." In other words, it is best to know what the reality truly is, so you know how to respond accordingly. In this sense, it should be noted that Eve was the one who chose to gain the knowledge of what the deal of existence was, through and through. Don't we all want that knowledge even now?

Is it fair to argue that the story of Adam and Eve and the forbidden fruit might not be a story about the coming of sin into the world, but the emergence of self-consciousness, and confronting the realities of the human situation.

One worthwhile theme to gain from this story is that all knowledge carries with it a certain responsibility. You can hardly be held responsible for what you do not know, but you are responsible for what you do know, including the realization that there is more to know. Eve took all the risks in this story. It cost her—she lost something, she gained something. It is not easy living responsibly with the things we know. What we learn from Eve is that any paradise based upon ignorance or half the truth, is fool's gold.

Eve might have been the first rule-breaker, but the most notorious rule-breaker of all time has to be Jesus.

People often envision Jesus as someone tiptoeing around in a flowing robe, speaking softly, patting children on their head, and carrying a baby lamb in his arms. But the real Jesus of history was a lightning rod. He was the greatest debunker of religious hierarchies and traditions, and the greatest desacralizer of holy places, times, people, rituals, and priests that this world has ever seen. The religious establishment hurriedly condemned him to death for blasphemy, while the secular powers executed him for sedition. Jesus opposed, challenged, confronted, subverted, and undermined the religious and societal systems and structures of his day. Jesus would not back down or go away. He defied the old order and called for a new one.

Jesus was not a Christian. He is not the founder of Christianity. Why? If Christianity is a religion, then Jesus certainly did not come to start one! It is doubtful Jesus would be a Christian were he alive today. Christianity IS a religion created in the name of Jesus and is often much different from the actual truth that Jesus taught and lived. The "Jesus" you often find in church is an edited, altered, adapted, refashioned, adulterated version. Richard Le Gallienne wrote, "Organized Christianity has probably done more to retard the ideals that were its founder's than any other agency in the world." It is often the case that you must disentangle Jesus from institutional Christianity in order to uncover his truth.

The pastor found a way at the end of his sermon on sin to tie in the resurrection, which he said was proof positive that Jesus is worthy to be our Savior and Lord. After a lengthy altar call and the closing *Because He Lives* hymn, the Easter service concluded. We piled back into the car, did Mexican for lunch, and hit the slopes.

The next morning, I went for a brisk walk; there are a lot of running trails in and around Arnold. As I was walking down the road to one of the trailheads, the woman who I had previously met in the street a couple of days prior was in her front-yard tending to her flowerbeds. When she spotted me coming, she stopped and greeted me. She asked, "How is your visit going?" I told her we had been doing a lot of skiing, and that we had attended an Easter Sunday church service at a local church. To which she replied, "I used to go to church." Shocker!

The woman went on to explain that she had been excommunicated for having a divorce. This now 67-year-old had married a man who sunk deeply into alcoholism. She held on through five children but when the kids were gone, she could endure no more, and filed for divorce. The church she attended held that adultery was the only scripturally justifiable grounds for divorce. She was instructed to work out the problems with her husband. When she went ahead with the divorce, it was viewed as disobedience to God, the Bible, and pastor authority, and she was punished by expulsion from the church. She was a rule breaker and paid the price. I could feel her sadness and bitterness as she shared her story. I was glad she didn't go to the church we went to on Easter.

Too often Christian religion is obsessed with "sin," and its entire message revolves around it. It proclaims a sin-management gospel. The main message too many people hear in church is, "You are not enough. You do not measure up. You fall short. God does not approve." It is a message of guilt and shame.

Back in Jesus' day, people walked away from religion, feeling there was no chance of ever being enough for God, but they walked away from Jesus feeling they were okay just the way they were. People walked away from religion under the weight of being "sinners," "filthy rags," undeserving, unworthy, and perpetually falling short in God's eyes, but walked away from Jesus feeling accepted and loved, and entertaining the possibility that maybe they were not so bad after all.

People walked away from religion with more rituals to observe, more rules to follow, more laws to keep, and more teachings to understand in order to get it right with God, but people walked away from Jesus feeling that they could simply live a life of love as he did, and that there was nothing more important than this, and it had to start with loving themselves.

You are never going to truly get to the liberating truth of Jesus unless you break a multitude of religious rules. I think religious folk edited out a section of Jesus' Sermon on the Mount. I'd put money on that one of them was,

"Blessed are the rule breakers."

CHAPTER 14

LESSONS FROM
THE DESERT

Off-road motorcycle riding has been a passion of mine for over thirty years. My dirt bike dreams have taken me across the wildest trails in California, Texas, Colorado, Washington, Idaho, Nevada, New Mexico, Utah, Oregon, and Montana, as well as numerous adventures throughout Baja Mexico. Five other men and I once rode across the Australian Outback, avoiding crocodiles and dodging kangaroos.

I also enjoy riding a street bike and recently six men and I rode 1800 miles of the German, Swiss, Italian, and Austrian alps slicing through 22 switchback-laden mountain passes. Cracking the throttle is my cathartic release of post-traumatic stress that builds up as a first responder.

Being present in the moment was not something I learned at a meditation retreat, but from all-terrain riding. You must block everything else out, focus, and apply your skills to stay alive. My favorite riding terrain is remote single-track trails that are technical and challenging. "Riding in the zone" means relaxing into the motorcycle, keeping your eyes up and ahead, and becoming one with the rhythm, contour, and pulse of the trail. Off-road riding brings the zone experience to a whole new level of alertness. Any significant lapse in focus could mean careening down a steep slope with the only thing stopping you from a long descent are stands of trees.

One of my greatest accomplishments in life was coaxing my entire family into becoming dirt bike enthusiasts. I managed to convince my wife Heidi into riding on our second date with the promise of a Jamba Juice *Peanut Butter Moo'd* smoothie. Yesterday, my son and I did a 60-mile ride in the Mendocino National Forest in Northern California.

There is nothing like going off-road in Baja, Mexico. It is a well-known region for adventure riding enthusiasts, especially since the mid 60's when the Baja 1000 became a world-renowned off-road motorsport race. The race allows several types of motor vehicles to compete on the same course with classes for cars, trucks, motorcycles, ATVs, and buggies. The record for a motorcycle is sixteen hours, 23 minutes, and 26 seconds.

The Baja 1000 is considered by many to be the most grueling, challenging, and craziest off-road race the world has to offer. The threats of dust storms, remote desert terrain, equipment failure and even death are just a few of the hazards challengers face each year. The Baja region of Mexico has a definite element of danger and risk. It is a desolate country with towns few and far between. Finding fuel must be calculated into your planning when travelling long distances. If something goes wrong, you must be prepared to improvise and do what it takes to remedy a problem.

As if the remoteness and natural dangers of the Baja 1000 were not enough, each year crazed spectators build actual booby traps for their "entertainment." The hazards have ranged from pits to barbed wire, and it is an extremely dangerous thing that some spectators do not seem to care about. As a rider, one must always keep their wits about them .

I had to learn about the perils of off-road riding in Baja for myself. One of those occasions I broke my collarbone in a remote area of Baja and had to ride my motorcycle 200 miles in excruciating pain to get back to my vehicle at the border. But this pales in comparison to what happened when me and eleven other men did a four-day Baja ride together.

Every Baja ride I have done has involved my friend Curt, who knows the region and all the trails like the back of his hand. With him along we can ride and not worry about getting lost. You do not want to get lost in Baja!

On this trip Curt led us twelve riders down Baja to a small town called San Felipe on the Sea of Cortez. Part of the deal on this trip was that Curt had to come back early and we assured him we could retrace our route and return to the border on our own. He was hesitant to leave us, but we insisted. He warned us, "You make one wrong turn and you will be screwed!"

The Baja region, particularly around the border, is fraught with risk and danger. Cabo San Lucas, a resort city on the southern tip of Mexico's Baja California peninsula, had a higher per capita homicide rate than any other city in the world, increasing by 500 percent from the previous year to 365 killings. The new U.S. travel advisory recommends "caution" to Baja California visitors. The statement says that "criminal activity and violence, including homicide, remain an issue." No, the Baja desert is not the place you want to get lost!

Curt left and we stayed another two days riding in the region. Our group of eleven started our journey back to the border, which should have been a five-hour ride. Typical Baja, the dust was kicking up and swirling, and we spread out to avoid eating each other's dirt. We rode in a line about 5 miles long from front to back. I was near the back of the pack, and we were all trusting that the lead rider knew the correct route. There were several turns along the way, and it was imperative to know which ones to make.

I bet you know how this story goes.

Sure enough, I made a turn following the line of riders in front of me. From what I remembered the turn did not seem right but it was not possible to go fast enough to catch the front of the pack. These riders were flying, a grade above what I could do on my bike.

I had a sick feeling.

As we rode on, I was certain we made a wrong turn. I also knew this was going to turn out bad. There were only two places where we could get fuel along the right way back. Unfortunately, our wrong turn meant no places to fuel up. We had climbed and descended a small mountain range into an expansive desert where one by one we started to run out of gas spread out over miles.

Not good.

Some guys had larger tanks and backtracked, siphoning gas so that we could all regroup. I will never forget after coming back together, realizing that we were out of gas in the middle of a remote and desolate desert as far as the eyes could see, with only an hour or so of daylight left. We were in big trouble. Our wrong turn could prove to be a fatal mistake in the Baja desert.

The winter temperatures dropped, and it began to drizzle as the sun faded from the sky. We were lost, out of gas, and in the middle of nowhere. This was not a staged sixth-season *Survivor: Baja* episode. This was a we-may-not-get-out-of-here-alive deal.

Meanwhile, the lead rider who got us all lost, who conveniently had a gas tank twice the size of the rest of us, took off leaving us stranded. I never rode with him again. We barely got a tiny fire going and tried to put our heads together to make a plan. After much deliberation into the night we agreed we would put all our remaining gas into one motorcycle in the hopes that the rider could reach someone to offer us help. We decided we would try to catch a some sleep and send him off at daybreak. I had visions of tarantulas and rattles snakes plotting to attack me in my sleep.

There is barrenness and emptiness in the desert. The darkness is heavy and absolute. It was like you just disappeared, vanished, and carried away by the winds. You feel insignificant and forgotten beneath the vast and unforgiving desert sky. Despite being in the company of nine other men, I felt alone, small, and helpless. It was one of the longest, coldest, darkest, tense, and scariest nights of my life.

The sun finally appeared. Our rider headed off. The plan worked, barely. About the time his gas tank went empty, he happened upon two Mexican men in a desert shack. They drove him to another shack where there was gas. I will never forget the sight of him rolling back into our little camp with two five-gallon gas cans on his lap. That supplied enough fuel to find our way back to the border.

It is curious that despite the barrenness, exile, and harshness of the desert, it has also come to represent the attainment of clarity, revelation, wisdom, and transformation. The desert has long played a significant role in religious traditions and individual awakenings. Much of the formative historical events in the Jewish tradition took place in or around deserts. A critical stage of Jesus' spiritual development happened after he was baptized and retreated to the desert.

The early history of the Christian faith includes the Desert Fathers and Mothers who lived as hermits in the deserts of Egypt, beginning in the third century AD. The desert became a place of solitude, surrender, and deep reflection. The Desert Fathers were convinced that the desert was the best place for encountering the presence of God. A collection of wisdom from some of the early desert monks and nuns is contained in the book, *Sayings of the Desert Fathers*.

Desert Father St. Isaac the Syrian wrote, "A man can never learn what divine power is while he abides in comfort and spacious living."

The wisdom here is recognizing that we as human beings strive to organize our lives around comfort, predictability, continuity, security, and familiarity. There is no shame in that. Who does not want to cultivate a life with the greatest possible equanimity and ease? No one goes out looking for turmoil, volatility, conflict, and uncertainty. However, the downside to doing our lives entirely in our comfort zone is that the challenges, stress, and tribulations in life is what inevitably calls forth and activates our higher God-given potentialities, or what St. Isaac called "divine power."

There must be an occasion involving fear, risk, doubt, or danger in order to draw forth and activate the part of who we are as courage. It is in situations that need or demand a response that tests the limits of your capability, power, and tenacity, that strength awakens and develops. Getting along with people we like or loving the significant others in our lives is doable but refusing to do harm and choosing goodwill toward people we do not like or hurt us, is how true compassion grows. Though no person hopes for tragedy, loss, and heartache, we also know that the painful events we experience often cause us to appreciate the gift of life more deeply and live it more intentionally.

The desert is a discomforting but fitting image for transformation. Sometimes life becomes barren, desolate, lonely, and dark. One minute you can be motoring along just fine in life, and suddenly all it takes is a bad turn and we are struck down by tragedy or loss. Our lives are stripped bare. We feel isolated, small, forgotten, and lost. We find ourselves in the middle of nowhere, feeling helpless and afraid. We see no way forward through our pain.

Every scene I arrive at as a first responder chaplain is a desert. Someone is stranded in a wasteland of heartache. They are harshly confronted by the severe realities of human existence. There is no relief for their sorrow. The certainty, stability, and security of their lives are swept away by a blinding sandstorm of grief, anguish, and fear. Tragedy and loss make life feel inhabitable. Each hour is a fight to stay alive. It is often in these moments when people feel abandoned by God. We feel forsaken in the badlands of our suffering.

An interesting thing in the Bible is how often the stories involve God doing the miraculous in a desert. A couple million Israelites and their livestock wandered around lost in the desert for 40 years. And to think I felt desperate in the Baja desert for one night! And yet God got them through it. That is day after day for forty long years! God has proven he can get people through the desert.

The Song of Moses is the name sometimes given to the poem which appears in Deuteronomy 32:1–43 of the Hebrew Bible, which according to the Bible, was delivered just prior to Moses' death. In the poem, Moses looks back over the journey of his life and remembers God's unwavering love and provision. In Deuteronomy 32:10, Moses says, "He found us in a wilderness, a wasteland of howling desert. He shielded us, cared for us, guarded us as the apple of his eye."

Our planet exists with many kinds of terrains, including plateaus, mountains, plains, valleys, deserts, swamps, forests, tundra, oases, and flat and open grasslands. Likewise, the terrain of human existence varies considerably. Sometimes the landscape of our lives is lush and flourishing, other times it is barren and desolate. The human journey takes you up to the summit of deep joy and happiness, but also drives you down into the dark valley of despair. We have moments when we are looking out across the open plains of inspiring possibilities, but then moments we feel defeated at the bottom of a mountain that looks impossible to climb. Sometimes life is a familiar and peaceful walk along a wooded trail, sometimes it is being lost and stranded in a desert. Wrong turns happen.

There are two things I have learned about God and life. The first one is that God never promised that my life would only involve the terrain I prefer. The second is that whatever the terrain, God is always there. Though it sure seems this way at times, I am never actually lost. God takes no wrong turns.

In the Book of Psalms, David expressed this same understanding with these words,

"Where can I go from your Spirit?
 "Where can I flee from your presence?
 If I go up to the heavens, you are there;
  if I make my bed in the depths, you are there.
 If I rise on the wings of the dawn,
  if I settle on the far side of the sea,
 even there your hand will guide me,
  your right hand will hold me fast.
 If I say, "Surely the darkness will hide me
  and the light become night around me,"
 even the darkness will not be dark to you;
  the night will shine like the day,
  for darkness is as light to you."

Where is God? He is everywhere you are.

I spent a chunk of years of my life always wanting different circumstances. I imagined everything would be better if I could just change the terrain. Eventually I discovered that the problem was not the circumstances themselves, but not knowing how to be in the circumstances I had.

The Indian monk, Shantideva, wrote,

"Where would I find enough leather
 To cover the entire surface of the earth?
 But with leather soles beneath my feet,
 It's as if the whole world has been covered."

You have two choices. One choice is to spend your life trying to make the circumstances of life what you want them to be. You can require, demand, and expect life to show up how you want it. The second choice is being able to find peace and contentment in any circumstance, whether it is the mountaintop of the desert. Saint Paul wrote, "I know what it is to be in need, and I know what it is to have plenty. I have learned the secret of being content in any and every situation, whether well fed or hungry, whether living in plenty or in want."

So, what is the secret?

It is what lies within you. Paul found inside him a "divine power" that Desert Father St. Isaac the Syrian alluded to when he wrote, "A man can never learn what divine power is while he abides in comfort and spacious living." You may never really know that you are never truly alone in this world until you are lost and stranded in a desert of loss. Do not be surprised if you discover a strength you did not think you had while standing at the foot of a Mount Everest challenge. Albert Camus wrote, "In the midst of winter, I found there was, within me, an invincible summer. And that makes me happy. For it says that no matter how hard the world pushes against me, within me, there's something stronger—something better, pushing right back."

There is a hope and faith that does not mean a whole lot when life is humming along as expected, which you discover in the valley of suffering is indestructible. Eventually you learn that at that very moment when you feel most forsaken by God, it is when he is there, with you, the apple of his eye.

While my motorcycle buddies and I were lost in the Baja desert we debated whether is was better to be lost in the middle of a cold brutal winter or a deadly hot summer. We wondered if in summer we could find water by digging deep enough into the ground. The consensus was that we could not. Out of curiosity, once the whole ordeal was over, I investigated it. Turns out, there are water tables everywhere, even in deserts. In the Sahara there are entire cities that depend on groundwater. How deep the water table is, depends on many variables. It could be 15 feet, 1,500 feet, or 15,000 feet below the surface. We are all familiar with a mirage as an optical illusion caused by atmospheric conditions that create the appearance of a sheet of water in a desert. But there is another kind of mirage in which it appears that the desert is anhydrous, holding no water, when in fact it does.

Maybe everything we need to walk through any situation in life, is within us, even if we have to dig a little to find it. The Spirit of God meets mankind most assuredly in the soul. Antoine de Saint-Exupery wrote, "What makes the desert beautiful is that somewhere, it hides a well."

CHAPTER 15

GOD WORKS
IN ~~MYSTERIOUS~~
HUMAN WAYS

May 8 started out like any other day at San Ramon Valley High School, an upper-middle-class National Blue-Ribbon public school in the East Bay area of San Francisco. I coach boys' volleyball at the school, and my youngest son is a student. Spring fever was in the air, and the anticipation for summer vacation was on everyone's mind with only a couple of weeks of classes left.

Fifteen year old freshman Benjamin Curry shouted goodbye to his mom and dad as he dashed through the kitchen to catch the school bus with his backpack slung over his shoulder, and a half-eaten granola bar in his hand. "Don't forget to talk to Miss. Franklin about your creative writing project!," Ben's mom shouted as he bolted out the door.

That was the last time Karen and Thomas Curry would ever see their son.

In Ben's fourth period Phys Ed class students had been developing their swimming skills and stamina through the practice of treading water. This is the ability to keep your head above water in an upright position by bicycling your legs while moving your hands back and forth. Even young children learn to tread water. It builds confidence. If you know that you can stay safe in deep water, you are more likely to feel calm and capable in the pool. It also helps swimmers conquer their fear of the "deep end" once they know that they will be able to stay afloat by treading water. This skill is not only essential for more advanced athletes and a superior fitness exercise to burn calories and fat, it is critical for basic water safety.

In a typical physical education class, students might be told to swim out to a lane line in the middle of the pool, and then push off from the line to tread water. The instructor uses a stopwatch to time the students, gradually increasing the duration, starting with thirty seconds, then one minute, three minutes, and so on. Treading water in a public school swim class happens without incident countless times every year across the US. But there are some risks. Floating on the back is the easiest way to achieve buoyancy in the water. Using muscles to propel the body upward to tread water is much more demanding. Swimming face-first in the water is the most natural way for people to swim, not staying in an upright position.

There were 57 students in Ben's fourth period physical education class treading water on May 8th. The instructor told the students they were going to be treading water in the pool for three minutes. He warned them if they touched the lane line, he would extend the time. So, when a student grabbed the line the teacher shouted that he was adding another thirty seconds, which would have made the total treading water time three minutes and thirty seconds.

While the students continued treading water, the instructor stood on a diving board. The extended time he added continued as he was looking at his cell phone and had now reached four minutes. It was during that extra time that Ben became exhausted and slipped underwater unnoticed and drowned in the 12-foot-deep pool.

The instructor recessed the class at the end of 4th period and gave a cursory check to make sure that all his students had safely left the pool but somehow missed seeing his student at the bottom of the pool. Ben was discovered after lunch had ended and students in the 5th period PE class entered the pool. A different instructor taught that class, and when she saw the boy at the bottom of the pool, she dove in and pulled Ben's body to the surface.

Ben was hauled from the water around 1:40 p.m. School staff, law enforcement and fire officials attempted lifesaving measures and Ben was rushed to Kaiser Walnut Creek Medical Center where he was pronounced dead.

Meanwhile, San Ramon Valley High School was thrown into turmoil as word quickly spread. Students and teachers were in shock that this had happened during a school class. The news media soon got a hold of the incident. Their vans seized the front of the school and media helicopters flew overhead, while police were carrying out their investigation.

That afternoon I was visiting with a group of firefighters at San Ramon Valley Fire Station #34 when I received a call-out from dispatch about a 15-year-old student who had drowned at the high school. My heart sank and realized it could be a student that I coached or knew. I at once drove to Kaiser Walnut Creek, where I was told the boy was being transported. I arrived before Ben's parents Thomas and Karen, learned that Ben had been pronounced dead. I found myself standing at the foot of Ben's lifeless body contemplating how this day was going to go.

Even though I did not know Ben or his parents, the fact that I was a coach at San Ramon Valley High School and one of my children was a student, helped in making an immediate connection with Ben's mom and dad. As agonizingly unthinkable it is that you could send your child off to school just like every other day and then be told it was his last day, it is equally inconceivable that your child could die at school. It is too much for any person to absorb. Ben was dead but the details surrounding his death were not yet entirely clear. Drowning? In Phys Ed class? How? No one saw him? Where was the instructor? No classmates noticed? Catastrophic heartbreak and anguish were compounded by confusion, disbelief, and anger.

Of all the tragedies that I encounter as a first responder chaplain, the most heartbreaking have been when parents have to deal with the death of a child. A child's death is especially traumatic because it is typically unexpected. It is a violation of the usual order of things, in which the child is expected to bury the parent. Studies that have compared responses to different types of losses have found that the loss of a child is followed by a more intense grief than the death of a spouse or a parent. Integrating the loss of a child into one's life narrative, making sense and new meanings of such a wrenching event, presents a daunting challenge to parents and family. Many parents share that their grief continues throughout their lives, often saying, "It gets different, it doesn't get better." Words such as "closure" can be deeply offensive.

There are some common components in grieving the death of a child. The first involves accepting the loss, facing the reality that the child is not going to return. The bereaved parents may vacillate between belief and disbelief. Rituals such as funerals aid with this task, and those who do not attend the funeral may have to find alternate ways to accept the reality. The period of shock associated with a child's death often lasts four to six weeks or longer.

Another aspect is processing the pain and it is this process, which is essential for the grieving parent to move forward. Grieving catastrophic loss is not simply a matter of the passage of time. It involves more deliberate steps that are critical. This pain is both emotional and physical and affected by internal and external (social) interactions. If people avoid dealing with the pain, it may manifest in depression later in life and become more complex to address.

A third component involves parents adjusting to a world without their child. This adjustment is linked to the ability to make meaning from the child's death. Evidence for the relevance of meaning making as a predictor of bereavement outcome is well established. Failure to adopt a constructive interpretation of the death of a loved one predicts heightened distress, particularly in the early months of grief. The inability to make sense of the loss is associated with protracted chronic grief trajectories, and a near-perfect predictor of violent bereavement through suicide, homicide, and accident. Identity change from the death of a child can precipitate a significant reorganization of one's sense of self, for better or worse. Bereavement research shows that the quest for meaning in loss is a crucial factor in grief recovery.

Maintaining a continuing bond with the deceased child is another part of the grieving process. Referred to as "continuing bonds," the bereaved parent finds a place for that relationship in their new life without the child physically present. Rather than being told to "let go," "move on" or "detach" from their child's death, they are encouraged to find meaningful ways for cultivating a continuity in the remembrance, appreciation, and connection with the child's life.

The grief process is multifaceted and complex. It is not tidy and linear and has no standard timetable. Grief is visceral, not reasonable; the howling at the center is raw and real. It obliterates the dailiness of life. Sorting out grief cannot be forced. There are milestones and setbacks. It is impacted by a multitude of factors and is different for every person. A central aspect of my work as a chaplain is connecting the grieving parents with community and professional resources to aid and support them through the grieving process.

As a first responder chaplain, when I am on the scene of a tragedy involving a child's death, I often find myself in that discomforting space that involves making sense of it. There is nothing that feels more senseless, indefensible, and beyond explanation than the unexpected death of a child. This is often where God comes up. Where is God? Why would God allow this? How could God take my child? These are frequent questions a chaplain is asked by a parent in acute grief. They are questions for which all my seminary-constructed theological answers seem woefully inadequate.

At San Ramon Valley High School, grieving students spontaneously created a makeshift memorial along the fence that enclosed the pool where Ben had drowned. Classmates and teachers left flowers and pinned handwritten messages and posters on the rail. Some left lit candles, and other objects. Ben played basketball and his teammates lined up their basketball sneakers along the fence.

That evening I received a call from the school asking if I would help organize a vigil to give students the opportunity to express their pain and grief. We decided to have the vigil the next night at the football stadium. That night over 1500 students, teachers, parents, and community members packed the stadium at San Ramon Valley High School with an overflow crowd of people standing where they could. There was a reverent, somber, and heavy-hearted spirit as people filed into the bleachers. The student body sat together, holding hands.

The vigil began with a song from the school choir, as students and teachers held candles that glowed in the darkness in remembrance of Ben. Two of his school friends paid tribute to Ben by sharing what he had meant to them. One friend shared a funny story about Ben's first day of freshman year when he managed to turn over the entire cart of stacked lunch trays in the school cafeteria that went crashing all over the floor, and just nonchalantly walked away like nothing happened. It received a roar of laughter in the crowd, but then quickly fell silent as the boy was suddenly overcome by sadness and tears began trickling down his face.

One of the teachers who spoke, had tragically lost her freshman daughter in a drowning ten years earlier. Shedding her own tears as she addressed the crowd, she shared how devastating and dark those days were, and the struggles and challenges of her grieving process. She shared that it eventually lead her to a place in which she not only grieved her, but felt deep gratitude to have had the privilege of loving her. She said to this very day she has never stopped loving her daughter. Sometimes only someone else who has experienced a similar loss can speak into the lives of those who are grieving. I wondered how Tom and Karen were impacted by her words. She told students that Ben would always be alive in the memories and hearts of those who knew him.

Finally, I was given the opportunity to speak. When I stepped behind the lectern, the first people I noticed were Ben's mother and father. I was surprised they had come. My last conversation with them was that they had planned to remain at home to begin contacting family members and make arrangements for Ben's funeral. The thought of attending the school vigil was more than they felt emotionally capable of doing. I supported their desire for privacy and personal space to absorb and grieve their loss. Something must have changed their minds to have chosen to attend.

I learned in my conversations with them at the hospital that Tom and Karen Curry were not members of any local faith community or active participants in any faith tradition. They mentioned that at one time years ago they had attended a church in the area but were no longer active.

San Ramon Valley High School is a public school. One of their central values is inclusivity, and they are proud of the accepting and supportive environment they have cultivated for LGBTQ+ students.

I am a chaplain, which means most people assume that there is some religious or aspect of God involved in the work I do. For this reason, it was unexpected that I was specifically asked to speak at Ben's vigil.

I shared briefly with the students about my work as a first responder chaplain, and how it takes me into traumatic situations of tragedy, heartbreak, and grief, like the devastating drowning and death of Benjamin Curry. I mentioned that in my work as a chaplain, I hear a lot of interesting things said about God, one of which is the well-known phrase, "God works in mysterious ways." I shared that one thing I had learned from twenty-five years as a first responder chaplain on the frontline of life's tragedies could be summed up in a different phrase, "God works in human ways."

Sometimes we imagine that the comfort, love, compassion, strength, support, relief, and help we need is far removed from us. The religious mindset locates them in a "God" somewhere up in heaven. But what good are they up there? The whole point of Jesus was showing that these transcendent realities are present and suitable for expression in and through human beings. I shared with the students that in the wake of Ben's death this would be a season of grief and sorrow. First and foremost, for Tom and Karen Curry and their family. I acknowledged that all those who knew Ben as friends and classmates, and the entire student body, faculty, and administrators at San Ramon Valley High School, will have their own grief and sorrow. I encouraged the students to consider that not one of us will be alone in our pain and sadness, and that we will carry and walk through it as one family.

I challenged the students to realize that even as they grieve, each of them can be expressions of comfort, compassion, strength, and support to one another. That whatever one's beliefs or faith may be, we can all agree that actively caring for one another fulfills any understanding of God or worthwhile philosophy of life.

Christian mystic, Teresa of Avila, wrote, "Christ has no body now but yours. No hands, no feet on earth but yours. Yours are the eyes through which he looks compassionately upon this world. Yours are the feet with which he walks to do good. Yours are the hands through which he blesses all the world. Yours are the hands, yours are the feet, yours are the eyes, you are his body. Christ has no body now on earth but yours."

Like Ben's parents, I have countless times heard people tell me about how they used to go to church and lost any real meaningful connection with God. I sometimes wonder if this would be different if churches spent less time worshipping Jesus and more time being Jesus to each other. In those moments when people are devastated by tragedy, they do not need a theological explanation but a real connection with empathy, kindness, grace, solidarity, and love.

One of my favorite Bible stories about Jesus is when he confronts a group of religious leaders who plan to stone a woman to death as a result of being caught in the act of adultery, which was punishable by stoning according to their religious law. After Jesus sends these men packing by saying that only a perfect law-keeper was qualified to cast a stone, he knelt in the dirt to tend to the woman. It is noteworthy what Jesus does not do. Jesus does not pray that the woman will discover and know the love of God. He did not crack open the Hebrew Bible to recite verses and stories about God's love. Jesus did not instruct the woman to meditate on a mountaintop or start a daily quiet time in order to experience God's love. He did not give her a pamphlet, "The Four Laws for Accessing Divine Love." No, Jesus did none of that. What did he do? Jesus knelt in the dirt and expressed love and compassion himself.

After more than two decades of being a first responder chaplain, here is what I've learned. For many years I wanted to save the world. I told people God loved them. But I was disappointed. The world did not change. Then one day I decided to stop telling people this, and just love them myself. This made all the difference. Telling people that God loves them is good theology, but loving them yourself is what transforms people's lives. The church is always wanting to "save" the world. But the world doesn't want to be saved, it wants to be loved. And that's how you save it.

After I spoke, I invited everyone down to the football field to mingle, embrace one another, and just be together. In the midst of the harrowing and heartrending death of Ben Curry, something beautiful, spontaneously came to life on that football field among these students.

Fyodor Dostoevsky wrote, "The darker the night, the brighter the stars. The deeper the grief, the closer is God." How could God get any closer than being present in and through each of us to one another? All this time we have been looking for God somewhere up in the sky, not realizing that God is present in our connectivity with one another. Looking across the football field at San Ramon Valley High School, I clearly saw that in those moments when we find ourselves in greatest need, God works in human ways.

CHAPTER 16

CHURCH IS NOT THAT

Alfred Tennyson wrote, "The churches have killed their Christ." This sentiment touches upon the discomforting truth that organized Christianity may be guilty of not living up to the truth that its founder taught and lived. Leo Tolstoy, wrote in *The Kingdom of God is within You*, "The Christian churches and Christianity have nothing in common save in name."

I've mentioned throughout this book that it is a common occurrence that when I arrive at a tragic scene as a first responder chaplain, people tend to associate the term "chaplain" with religion and God, and will often mention, "I used to go to church." But given the concerns such as Tennyson and Tolstoy raise, it is difficult to know exactly what any person might have learned about God and Christianity in church.

The phrase "used to go to church" implies a particular understanding of church, namely that it is a place you "go to." People often ask, "Where do you go to church?" which identifies church as a location, building, organizational identity, and a specific group of people who attend there. A denomination. A sect. A person may answer by saying something like, "I go to Hillsong Church near Union Square" or "I go to St. Mary's Catholic Church in Walnut Creek."

Church as a location and organizational identity can have a downside. I know from having been a church pastor myself. If you are not careful, you may start thinking that Christianity is something that mostly happens in church services, classes, meetings, events, and programs. The "Christian life" becomes Sunday mornings and Wednesday nights. Most churches have paid pastors, administrators, teachers, and ministry leaders, which can sometimes create a spiritual hierarchy of "clergy" (God professionals) and "laity" (God amateurs). People learn to give preference to those with bible degrees and paid church positions. The pastor(s), staff, leaders, and elders are considered to be closer to God than the rank-and-file church member.

As a church pastor, I spent a lot of time with other clergymen and leaders at conferences about how to effectively build, lead, and grow a church. There are some pitfalls one can easily tumble into. I learned that church "success" is often defined by numerical growth. At pastor conferences the question was always, "How big is your church?" No one ever asked about the transformation of people's lives. People with big churches were considered successful. You did not give the time of day to pastors of small congregations. I could name the top 5 churches in America and most people in Christian subculture could name the Senior Pastor. The next best thing to being a rock star is being the leader of the latest and greatest megachurch.

Being a pastor was my livelihood, and job security depended upon the success of our church. It does not take a rocket scientist to see that in these circumstances you might be prone to define and reward Christianity as participation in church structures and programs. But despite the pressure of increasing church attendance and membership, Christian living is fundamentally a lived experience and way of life, not a centralized or program-dependent phenomenon. It was not always easy keeping this straight.

There can also be a temptation to prefer style over substance and be concerned about the entertainment value of church services. As a pastor I always felt the need to be innovative and strive for novelty, which we referred to as being "relevant" and "cutting edge." This can lend itself to consumer spirituality, which commodifies God into a buffet of programs, classes, social events, and first-class website and social media presence.

There were times, as a church pastor, when I operated with blinders on. My goal was to build "my" or "our" church, never mind that Jesus' primary message was about the kingdom of God. I was sometimes so busy building our church realm that it never occurred to me to collaborate with other churches to be an expression of God's kingdom together in the area. Pastors can be the most territorial people.

Over the years I have talked with countless people who have attended many different kinds of churches—fundamentalist, progressive, huge churches, home churches, liturgical, and contemporary churches. Organized church can be controlling. You would think church members, if left to themselves, would be starting cult clubs at church if they were not kept in line with the policies, procedures and approved books and studies of the church. Church environments can also be superficial. Church folk may project an image of having it all together or being super spiritual, but masking the pain, brokenness, and dysfunction inside themselves and their lives. Meeting-based and surface-level relationships, which sometimes characterize institutional church, can often lack the depth, honesty, authenticity, and vulnerability that we need in our relationships to support our growth and transformation.

In my twenty-five years as a first responder chaplain I have also encountered many people who shared how their involvement in church and institutional Christianity was damaging and detrimental. Some told me how fear, guilt, and shame were used to engender

USED TO GO TO CHURCH

obedience and devotion to God. Others described an authoritarian and control-oriented style of church leadership where questioning the minister was the equivalent of questioning God. One person shared with me that their church was always emphasizing submission, loyalty, and obedience to those in authority. Asking controversial theological questions, expressing a dissenting view, or disagreeing with the political views of the church leaders was viewed as a rebellious spirit.

Some church-leavers spoke of the unrealistic expectations of their congregation involvement and financial giving, and how "accountability" was a mechanism of control. There were others who shared how their church would demonize "non-Christians", other churches, different religions, and "secular" fields of knowledge such as science and psychology, and culture that did not validate their particular beliefs or narrow view of the world.

Of course, this does not describe all church congregations or all those who have served in as pastors, leaders, staff members, and administrators. I know many churches that nurture a profound and meaningful spirituality in people's lives, create a community of authentic and substantial relationships, serve the needs of their neighborhoods, communities, and cities, and actively take up the cause of social justice.

The church historically has also had some dark moments. Throughout history, institutional Christianity has sadly rationalized practices such as: the persecution of heretics; misogyny; religious intolerance; institution of slavery; white supremacy; opposition to scientific progress; violence and war.

I sometimes wonder what aspects of Christianity Jesus would be unhappy about if he returned. What would make Mark Twain write, "If Christ were here there is one thing he would not be—a Christian"?

My lifelong experience in and with church has been full of mixed emotions. I was in church every Sunday, as long as I can remember.

My mother took my two younger brothers and me to the same Presbyterian church she had attended since her childhood. Dad did not attend church with us. He was raised a Greek Orthodox. The closest Greek congregation was some sixty miles away in Los Angeles. Dad was like the many people I meet as a chaplain who "used to go to church" but no longer had any real interest in attending. Though he was proud of being Greek and would not hesitate to claim his Greek Orthodox heritage, his association with God and religion revolved around church rituals, rites, routines, and regulations. He could talk about his church but had little to say about God experientially.

As my brothers and I got older, we started attending "big church," which was the adult worship service. It became torture to sit patiently through the service every Sunday. It was always the same. First came the invocation, the call to worship, a reading, the Gloria Patri, the Doxology, the sermon and finally, the benediction. It all seemed stuffy, formal, and rigid. If it is true that "the medium is the message" this was not a very promising portrayal of the Almighty. God seemed to be mostly about pomp and circumstance, and overly concerned about robes, rules, and rituals. The formality and ceremoniousness of the church made God seem distant, detached, and harsh. God was to be revered, feared, and obeyed... or else.

I closed the book on God throughout high school and college. It was the 60's, and there were more interesting and rebellious things to do. There was Beatlemania, Jimi Hendrix, hippies, counterculture movement, lava lamps, tie dye t-shirts, Wilma Rudolph, Johnny Unitas, and Dr. Strangelove. I met Jane Fonda, smoked pot with Hunter S. Thompson, and jumped into the middle of the social revolution with both feet. The 60's were also volatile and tragic. I lived through the assassinations of John and Robert Kennedy, Martin Luther King, Jr., and Malcolm X. There was the Vietnam War, Cuban Missile Crisis, race riots, and Charles Manson.

In a Rolling Stone interview, Jerry Garcia said, "The lame part of the Sixties was the political part, the social part. The real part was the spiritual." People think of the "spiritual but not religious" trend as a recent phenomenon, but I saw it born in the 60's. The change in disposition was revealed through the music of the time. John Lennon was imagining, "No need for greed or hunger, A brotherhood of man." People spoke of experiencing a tremendous lift during that period. There was an energy of love, authenticity, togetherness, and harmony that connected people together as never before. We felt the possibility that a whole new world could have opened up.

The Jesus People Movement was born out of the 60's. By the summer of 1967, nearly 100,000 hippies and counterculture kids had gathered in the Haight-Ashbury neighborhood of San Francisco where they soon experienced something even more revolutionary than "tuning out and turning on": a born-again religious conversion. The message that these countercultural "Jesus Freaks" delivered to their peers stood for a radically different version of Christianity than the one preached in most churches at the time. We repudiated institutional churches and their weak and vapid "Churchianity." Instead, we stressed the need for a personal relationship with Jesus, who in our telling, was not far from being a hippie himself.

The 1967 "Summer of Love" was a radical revolution of Jesus People who had come to serve the poor, bring about racial harmony, oppose war and violence, and challenge the political establishment. We hung out with outcasts, criminals, and prostitutes while leading an underground liberation movement for peace and justice. Jesus People communes and coffee houses multiplied in the Bay Area.

The spirit of the 60's left its mark on me. I experienced my own spiritual rebirth. Rather than opposing institutional religion and organized church from the outside, I decided to take up the cause of reforming it from the inside. Deciding to attend seminary for theological and pastor training, I discovered in my studies that the history of the Judeo-Christian tradition is firmly rooted in counter-cultural and revolutionary ethos, opposing dominant culture and institutional power.

The radical break of Moses and Israel from imperial dominance was a break from both the religious and political oppression of the Egyptian Empire. Moses was concerned with the formation of a counter community with a counter consciousness that nurtured, nourished, and evoked an alternative to the dominant culture. The alternative was a way of being in a world that was rooted in relationship with God. It involved setting up a new community which would be centered on God's freedom, justice, and compassion.

The Old Testament prophetic tradition continued this spiritual countercultural community and movement. The prophets challenged hearers to recognize that the activity of God in their midst demanded that they see the world in a new way. They aroused people out of complacency and numbness of mindsets, beliefs, narratives, and ideologies of dominant culture and oppressive systems of power. The prophets imagined a different self-understanding and God-understanding that could transform the very fabric of reality. They lit a fire among the people to expose, in words and deeds, the destructive nature of an Empire and declare their commitment to resist it with every spiritual resource at their disposal.

The prophetic tradition culminated in Jesus, who spearheaded a holy revolt against the religious and political establishment and powers of his day. Jesus announced the inauguration of a new "kingdom" that was present within the human soul and carried with it the authority of God. He turned the dominant understanding of God on its head, accosted the religious establishment, and dismissed the Roman rule as bankrupt and powerless. Jesus cast a new vision for the world, where the last became first, and love was the only rule. The first followers of Jesus and the earliest Christian communities that formed after his death embodied this same revolutionary spirit of Jesus.

It is no mystery why Jesus would have been a universally compelling and galvanizing figure in the 60's. Jesus was the quintessential spiritual but not religious, anti-establishment, nonconformist, heroic, rebel-rousing, champion of the marginalized and oppressed, articulating a new vision of reality that John Lennon sang about.

It is unfortunate what the Christian church became. At the root, Christianity has always been a subversive and revolutionary force in the world—the party of overthrow, flatly denying that Caesar's will was the supreme law. But later Christianity was morphed into the state religion and lost the rebellious power it inherited from prophetic Judaism. The leader of the overthrow party, Jesus, was co-opted to become the posterchild for the Christian religion, a political maneuver by Constantine to consolidate his power. What an irony—the man considered public enemy #1 became their press secretary.

As described in the New Testament, church was never defined as a place, building or a denomination. The word "church" in the Bible is best interpreted into English as "the called-out ones." Church is people. People with a distinct way of being, people in dynamic relationship with one another and the world who embody and advance the revolutionary vision of Jesus for humankind.

Church is not fundamentally an organization with a name and 501c3 status. It is not something that happens at a specific location or inside a building. A house of worship is not essential to the true nature of a church. Christians did not begin to build church buildings until a couple of a hundred years after the death of Jesus.

In the early church, it was evident, by their ordinary life and interactions, who among them was living spiritual truth day in and day out. These individuals naturally emerged as encouragers, teachers and mentors. The truths Jesus taught and lived held sway over people's hearts, and they accepted that the life and spirit that Jesus displayed was within them, leading and guiding them forward. The early church was distinguished by the kind of relationships they had with one another,

Church is not an infrastructure that professional clergy and paid staff preside over and manage. It is not the configuration of worship service, classes, meetings, programs, events, and committees. The idea of a spiritual hierarchy of "clergy" and "laity," or a superstar pastor and paid staff team does not appear in the Bible. Instead, Paul spoke of the church functioning as a human body, where every person is equally important. The New Testament described church as people practicing "one-anothering" with each other—loving one another, caring for one another, serving one another, bearing one another's burdens, accepting one another, forgiving one another, encouraging one another, being honest and authentic with one another, respecting one another, listening to one another, living in harmony and goodwill with one another.

I am not saying that church buildings, pastors, paid ministry positions, worship services, and programs are wrong. I am simply expressing that they are not fundamentally what church is. Church may take any number of different forms. Most people who argue about church are erroneously equating their particular form of church as some sort of standard or ideal and preferable model that others should follow. Church is people identified by their way of being in the world and in relationship with one another. Regardless of how you do it, what constitutes church is relationships—with God, people, life, and the world. "Church" can be taking place in some form or fashion everywhere, all the time, with everyone.

With all those who have told me over the years as a first responder chaplain that they "used to go to church," I am saddened that they seem to think of church as a place you go or stop going. Why would someone deny themselves connection with a group of people who genuinely and actively accept, love, support, and care for one another in relationships of mutual trust, authenticity, vulnerability, and depth, and people who do life together through experiences and times of tragedy and triumph? Why would someone walk away from the most compelling, liberating, transformative, life-changing, and revolutionary vision for all of humankind and the world?

Maybe it is because they have never experienced what church really is.

My thinking about church has evolved over the years. I do not think of it as "going to church" but being the church. For me, church is not what you do at a particular location, but a way of being, specifically, a way of being with others. Every tragic scene I arrive at as a first responder chaplain is church. It is being that person who actively loves, serves and cares for another. It is being a representative of the greatest story ever told. It is my resistance against the dominant culture of fear, hopelessness, and despair. It is my commitment to the revolution "on earth as it is in heaven."

CHAPTER 17

IS THERE LIFE ~~AFTER~~

BEFORE DEATH?

"We need a chaplain for a 13-year-old suicide."

That dispatch call came to me as I was fixing a porch light at home on a sunny mild February day in the East Bay of San Francisco. I dropped everything and headed to the address given me contemplating how awful this incident will be. When I arrived, mom and son were home, sitting speechless on the couch in shock. Just thirty minutes earlier the mother had found her little girl dead. She hung herself with a belt in her room. Deputies were upstairs doing their investigation.

In the next 24 hours, close to 5,000 teens will attempt suicide and around 20 will be successful. Suicide is the 2nd leading causes of death for youth and young people between the ages of 12-24.

I introduced myself to the mother and her son, expressed my condolences, and explained that I would be on the scene to offer any support they needed. Most people don't know what the role of a chaplain is at a scene of tragedy and loss, and assume the chaplain is there to interject God and religion into the situation. As a first responder chaplain I am essentially performing psychological first aid and care for those devastated by tragedy or loss. In some cases, this may include giving aid and support to the first response team that is affected by the gruesome and disturbing aspects of a critical incident.

Obviously there is a spiritual component implied by the term "chaplain." Spirituality is a realm or area of inquiry that is non-material. It is being concerned with the human spirit or soul as opposed to material or physical things. EMS responders are typically responding to the physical aspects of a person's life and survival—mitigating physical trauma, providing medical intervention to serious bodily injuries, performing CPR, or other life-saving measures. My role as a chaplain is responding to the interior mental, emotional, and spiritual dynamics of those who are affected by these tragic scenarios.

At the most fundamental level, spirituality relates to a sense of connection to something bigger than ourselves. We often use words such as "sacred" or "transcendent" to describe spiritual experiences. Human beings need a framework of values, a philosophy of life, a religion or spiritual outlook to live and understand by—to make sense and find meaning in our lives and world. Spirituality exists wherever we struggle with the issues of how our lives fit into the greater scheme of things. We encounter spiritual issues every time we wonder where the universe comes from, why we are here, or what happens when we die. We also become spiritual when we become moved by values such as beauty, love, or creativity that seem to reveal a meaning or power beyond our visible world.

Spirituality reveals our personal desire to establish a felt-relationship with the deepest meanings or powers governing life. For me and many others, our spirituality is related to a belief in and relationship with God. Spirituality even involving God, however, doesn't necessarily have to be "religious" in the sense of being structured into rules, rituals, doctrines, and organizational activities.

Loss and tragedy puts our spirituality to the test. One's sense of meaning, equanimity, faith, and peace in times of relative ease and normalcy, can be shattered by unexpected tragedy and catastrophic loss. Though suffering confronts, tests and destabilizes our internal resources, it is often a door into a deeper spirituality. Spirituality is the most powerful force available for the transformation of human suffering. Out of suffering have emerged the strongest souls. Clive Barker wrote, "Any fool can be happy. It takes a human with real heart to make beauty out of the stuff that makes us weep."

One of my roles as a first responder chaplain is to look for natural ways that a person may connect with an aspect of spirituality to support and aid them in their grief and heartache. In my initial conversation with the mother and son on the couch I discovered that mom was an executive with a popular clothing company chain headquartered in the Bay Area. Here was a woman at the top of her career, life seemingly "good" and in an instant all the walls of "good" come crumbling down.

There was an urgent effort to contact the unaware father who had left earlier to run an errand. I was on the scene for about 20 minutes when suddenly the now informed dad came bursting through the front door. He ran straight through the foyer and up the stairs to his daughter's room where her dead body laid motionless on the floor in front of her bed. Whereas mom and son sat quietly in despair, the father had a deep visceral strong reaction kneeling at the side of his baby girl. From downstairs I suddenly heard yelling and screaming but it sounded more like an altercation was taking place with the several deputies who followed dad upstairs.

My reaction was to run upstairs because it sounded like all hell was breaking loose. At the sight of seeing his daughter all the father could think to do was to join his girl and he had the means to do so with a handgun in his bedroom closet down the hall. He ran to his bedroom with deputies close behind who were unaware of his plan until he got his hands on the gun at which time the deputies attempted to wrestle the gun out of his hands. I jumped into the fracas to aid in helping control the father. I'll never forget looking into the man's eyes and seeing a look that told me, "A part of this man just died." It was as if his soul left him and no doubt he felt that way. The deputies had no choice but to place him in the back of a patrol car out in front of the house until he calmed down. I got into the car with him to try and deescalate the situation.

As you can imagine the man was inconsolable in grief and despair. After a few minutes, his volatility turned into resignation. We began to talk. He could not come up with any reason whatsoever for why his little girl would take her life. She showed no signs of depression or other troubles and was a popular and talented young lady with many good friends. After a few moments of silence, he shared that his daughter was an honor student at school, but that morning had told him about a poor grade she was receiving in a class. He could not imagine that this would have been a reason she would have killed herself.

Parents like to think that they know what is going on with their children, and that they would know if their teen was suicidal. However, research shows that this is not always the case. In a study published in the journal *Pediatrics*, researchers interviewed more than 5,000 adolescents ages 11 to 17. In those interviews, they asked them if they had ever thought about killing themselves. The parents were asked if they believed that their teens had ever thought about killing themselves. Close to three-quarters of the parents of adolescents who said they had thought of killing themselves, said with certainty that their child had never contemplated suicide.

If you think about it, this is not very surprising, for lots of reasons. Teens may not always realize how bad they are feeling and may not want to tell their parents when they do. Parents may miss or misinterpret signs of depression in their teens. It is natural to want to believe that your child is fine, rather than thinking that they might be suicidal. Given how much drama can be intrinsic to the life of a teen, it is understandable that parents could misinterpret statements about death or dying as standard teen drama. And as it turns out, dropping grades at school is a common reason for anxiety and depression in teens that could be a trigger for suicide.

Later in our conversation, the father said something that I often hear in situations when a person's loved one has died. They are words often spoken in an effort to comfort and soothe oneself in a time of painful loss. He said, "I hope she's in a better place now."

It is hard to know exactly what he meant by this. Perhaps it expressed a firm belief he had about the afterlife. Maybe it was a hopeful sentiment in a moment of heartache that his daughter was now free from the emotional pain and struggle that led to her suicide.

Though each of the tragic situations I respond to as a first responder chaplain are different, most of them involve death. Except for a mortician and a coroner, there are few people who deal with death as a routine part of their job more than I do.

Fewer Americans say they believe in God; yet more people believe in an afterlife nonetheless. Eighty one percent of all Americans indicate that they believe in an afterlife of some sort. Over 70 percent of Millennials say they most definitely believe in life after death. The top afterlife beliefs include the Christian view of heaven and hell. Another common belief about the afterlife is that our physical components and life-energy are naturally scattered and return to the universe in some form. Reincarnation asserts that life after death involves the rebirth of the soul in a new body.

The hallmark of virtually all religions and philosophies is some belief about what happens after you die. The Christian religion often portrays the here life as an unfortunate reality we will one day be rescued from. The significance of Jesus is seen as the guy who punches your ticket to heaven. Beautiful mansions, streets of gold, the absence of all suffering, and eternal joy and happiness is God's reward for those who have faithfully endured the mess of this world. This is what we mean when we say things like, "At least they're in a better place now."

Whatever belief a person may have about life after death, there is no debate that every human being dies. Both celebrities and the unknown, wealthy and poor, Christians and Atheists, young and old, all die. Great heroes and wildly successful people die. Gifted and brilliant people die. Every enlightened monk, died. Every person Jesus healed, died. Buddha died. Jesus died. Every human being who has ever lived, currently living, or will live, will be met with the same fate of death. This includes you and I. Rarely do we know when or how, but this much is certain: whatever may happen after we die, this life we are now living will come to an end. As that great theologian Jim Morrison wrote, "No one gets out alive."

The ten-million-dollar question will always be: "Is there life after death?" People find refuge in religion because it claims with absolute certainty to have the correct answer. We cannot entirely know what happens after we die. We do not know what will happen an hour from now, much less what we will find after we die. All religious teachings and explanations are using words, explanations, descriptions, images, and figurative language to indicate a reality that is not of this world. These signifiers do not correspond exactly and perhaps not even roughly with the thing it claims to be signifying. As the saying goes, "When pointing at the moon, don't confuse your finger with the moon."

Over the years of my work as a first responder chaplain, I have shifted my mindset and focus from death to life. In every situation I am called into, there is nothing I or anyone else can do to change the tragic reality of someone's death. What can be done is tend to those who will continue living in their absence. I no longer think of the grieving process as simply processing death, but as an integral part to living more wholly and completely. Whether it is being fully present with acceptance and compassion to another human being who is pouring out their heartache and pain, or listening empathetically to a hurting soul doubt or curse God; or assisting a person with the practical matters related to the death of a loved one, or connecting them with resources for healing and recovery, I view everything I do as a first responder chaplain as supporting their ongoing journey of life after the death of a loved one.

People are often caught up in explanations, speculations, and debates about the question: Is there life after death? I wish more people had that same passion and vigor in addressing the question: Is there life BEFORE death? Having been close to death so often I can confess that death invokes more uncertainty than certainty.

E.M. Forster wrote, "Death destroys a man, but the idea of death saves him." In other words, death will one day take our life but knowing this compels us to embrace life more fully and with a greater sense of urgency and importance. This is a recurring theme in the Bible. Moses wrote in Psalm 90:12, "Teach us to number our days, that we may gain a heart of wisdom." King David in Psalm 144 wrote, "Man is like a breath; his days are like a passing shadow." James, the brother of Jesus, wrote in his New Testament Epistle, "You do not know what tomorrow will bring. What is your life? For you are a mist that appears for a little time and then vanishes."

A person can curse God because death is a reality of life, or they can be grateful that God let us know. What one *can* have is faith, hope and love centered on what we can know about God.

The parents asked me to officiate the memorial service for the 13-year-old girl who took her life. We have been friends to this day. I have shared their daughter's story in school auditoriums all over the region to well over 10,000 high school students. I am often asked to speak at suicide prevention events. It is always a bit of a shock when I begin my talk by telling students that I plan to give them ten reasons why their life is worth living. As a first responder chaplain addressing the subject of suicide, people are naturally expecting a lot of sobering talk about tragedy and death. But in my mind, the best way to address the subject of death is to talk about life, and the best way to prevent a teenager from giving up on living is to help them find reasons why they would not want to.

Jesus was always challenging people to find eternal life where they were. He was not shy about proclaiming that the best of God had already come. Jesus once told people that the kingdom of God had arrived. They scratched their heads in bewilderment and told Jesus they did not see it, to which Jesus replied they had to find it within themselves. The message of Jesus was that the best of all worlds was here and now, not somewhere else, and later. Jesus said that in every human being there is a special heaven, whole and unbroken.

Consider the possibility that we are never separated from God, which means we are never separated from life. In other words, God is the ground of all being. Everything finds its life in and through God. Whatever that may be after this earthly existence, the most real part of who we are always lives and never dies. Rather than guessing, arguing, and debating about what the afterlife entails, maybe we should instead focus on the here life we have now. As painful as her earthly absence is, that 13-year-old girl was not lost to death, she moved on to a different life. Whether it is on this side or that side, it is always life.

Seneca wrote, "Begin at once to live, and count each separate day as a separate life."

Here are the basic facts:

1. You have your life—the one you are living right now.

2. Once your lifetime is finished, whenever that might be, you can never have that life back.

3. You have already lived a number of years; but there is 100% of the rest of your life left.

4. Ask yourself: Is this the life I want to be living? Is this the person I want to be? Is my life an expression of what truly and deeply matters most to me?

5. Live that life.

What if God appeared to you one night and informed you that eternal life was this life, lived once again and innumerable times over again. In other words, eternal life was you living all the details of the life you have lived until now, over, and repeatedly forever. Does this thought experiment make you shudder, or would it be a source of comfort and joy? Would you receive this as good news or terrible news? Would you be grateful and celebrate, or gnash your teeth and curse God?

If the life you are currently living in terms of your daily choices, actions, mindsets, priorities, values, and commitments, is not something you would be inspired to live again and again and again for all eternity, maybe it's time to make a change.

Oscar Wilde wrote, "To live is the rarest thing in the world. Most people exist, that is all." We can get so wrapped around the axle of what kind of life we will after we die, that we do not truly live the life we have now.

CHAPTER 18

OUR FATHER

30,660 days
736,328 hours
706,406,400 breaths
3,528,000,000 heartbeats

That is the number of days, hours, breaths and heartbeats of a human being who lives to the age of 84. A lot happens in a person's life that spans over eight decades. It is a profound and sacred experience to be present when a person of this age arrives at their last day and hour, and final heartbeat and breath. I had the privilege of sitting beside a man to witness such a moment. I have never been the same since. I knew this individual well. The 84-year-old man was my dad.

It was the day before Christmas when my father was diagnosed with terminal cancer. The doctors gave him three to six months to live. Oddly enough, the day I received the call that my father was close to death, I had been dispatched to a scene where a man in his 80's had died in his home. His wife and daughter requested a chaplain. After being with this family for some time my phone rang, and I noticed it was my brother. I let it go to voicemail because I was engaged with this family, but I had a feeling it was something important related to our father. A few minutes later the phone rang again, and I answered.

My brother said that dad was not doing well and would not likely survive the day.

The week prior my mom had finally requested that hospice bring a hospital bed to our home in Southern California. Dad was having difficulty maneuvering in and out of bed. They put it in the family room where his special recliner had always been. Growing up, no one dared to sit in "dad's chair." It was an enduring family joke that he would specify in his legal will that he wanted to be buried in his recliner. Hauling it off and replacing it with a hospital bed was discomforting.

The family at the scene where I had been dispatched were very gracious when I explained my father's situation and needing to leave. I had to figure out how to go 450 miles from Northern to Southern California as quickly as possible. I managed to find a flight that was leaving Oakland in 90 minutes.

My 19-year-old daughter was at home and she drove me to the airport in tears knowing her grandfather was dying. As a first responder chaplain, every day I find myself in a tragic situation where people are suffering catastrophic loss and heartbreak, but this was the first time I can remember my daughter and I feeling deep grief and weeping together. Dad was a character larger than life to all seven of his grandkids with his gregarious personality and sense of humor. He loved his grandchildren and they were close to him in ways that even my brothers and I were not.

It was nothing short of a miracle that I was at my father's side three hours after getting the call from my brother. This was the only home I had ever known. It was the home of my childhood and youth, and the place I returned to visit after venturing off into adulthood and marriage. If those walls could speak, they would tell the story of a son with a strained relationship with his father.

Dad provided for his family and was a committed father and husband. I do not know that he missed a single sporting event of any one of his three sons, which included football, baseball, basketball, and track. We did a lot of fishing with dad, having grown up near the ocean and owning a small fishing boat. You could say dad was a family man, committed and loyal to his wife and kids. My father was known as a gregarious, good-natured, and well-liked person in the community. He was a mailman and everyone on the route he walked for many years knew and loved him. He would do anything for anybody who was in need. There were plenty of good reasons to love the man. And I did. So did a lot of people.

But my father was also a hard man. Growing up he was rigid, strict, and temperamental with us three boys of which I was the oldest. He could be tough on mom too. Dad seemed like an easy-going guy in public, but he ruled with an iron fist at home. My father had an anger problem. If you tripped the switch, he would explode. Though he was not physically abusive his verbal tirades were extreme. Being the oldest, much of his anger was directed at me. We had a volatile relationship as I grew older and more independent. Those sixties! Remember? It was "cool" to be rebellious and my dad made it easy to rebel. There were times it seemed we despised each other.

I will always remember him telling us how his Greek immigrant father, my grandfather, had a barber's blade sharpening belt made of thick leather, which was used on my dad and his three brothers for all kinds of infractions when they were children. Dad told us he once spent thirty days in his room because he wandered out of a dime store with a piece of gum without having paid for it. He always said that we should consider ourselves lucky that he did not use that sort of corporal punishment on us. Many years later, mom shared with me that she had threatened to leave him when I was a child because of the severity of a spanking that he had leveled upon me. She told him if he ever beat me like that again she would leave.

I eventually came to a fair view of my dad. A person can either canonize or demonize their father. No human being is all good or all bad, but a combination of them based upon countless factors and conditions, some of which are outside their control. The aspects of my father that I found hurtful were him repeating the same mindsets, behaviors, and wounds that he experienced with his own father. That does not excuse the ways my father hurt others, but it is a basis for understanding and compassion. When I grew up and became a father, I was shocked to discover that I was not perfect either or had my own issues to address.

It was not until my later adult years that I stopped deploring my father for who he was not and started appreciating him for who he was. George Herbert wrote, "One father is more than a hundred schoolmasters." The entirety of my relationship with my father, including the difficulties, struggles, and hardships, taught me something invaluable for my life's journey. He insisted upon the commitment, courage and resolve to realize our highest individual potential as men in the world, but he also showed us that this meant sacrificing ourselves to serve others and come to the aid of those in need.

God the Father is a title given to God in various religions, most prominently in Christianity. The title of Father has a privileged place in the Christian tradition because of its use by Jesus. There is no question that "father" is a complex metaphor for God. It is likely that a person who has adopted this metaphor will in some part project upon God the characteristics of and the nature of their relationship with their earthly father. The same would be true if Jesus has referred to God as "mother." If you think favorably of your mother and your relationship with her, you would likely have a more positive view of God, but if your mother was abusive, this could negatively impact your image of God.

In addition to "father", the Bible is filled with hundreds of metaphors for God, including: "shepherd", "rock", "sun", "shield", "creator", "light", "physician", "vine", "fire", "love", and "nursing mother". Why not choose a single metaphor to depict God in a straightforward and consistent fashion? Because there is no single comparison that can encapsulate all there is to say about God and the complexity of the divine-human connection.

God is neither man nor woman: God is God. We are told in the Bible, "God is spirit." God is often anthropomorphized in order to understand God in terms that are accessible to us as human beings. Ascribing maleness to God as "Father" is not meant to be understood as God having male sex organs, full beard, and lots of masculine testosterone.

God first appears in a parental role as the creator of Adam and Eve. God offers himself in loving relationship to them, cares for their well-being, and sets them up in an environment of security and flourishing. The use of the "father" metaphor for God in the context of historical Judaism meant God as Father to Israel. In other words, God is seen as Father and Israel as Son, specifying the special relationship between God and his chosen people. In the New Testament, God is depicted as Father to Jesus, the Son, once again depicting a special relationship. This idea is further expanded in the Bible into the concept of "sonship," which is the revelation that human beings are meant to understand their relationship to God through the framework of a loving and secure parent-child relationship.

No metaphor or anthropomorphism of God should be taken as a definitive explanation of God. When we use concepts, and figurative language to indicate God, we are referencing an ultimate reality that is beyond all words and mental formations.

That morning before I arrived, my father ate breakfast and suddenly slipped into a coma, precipitating my brother's call. By midafternoon, dad's breathing was slow and labored as I sat next to him holding his hand. It had only been a few months since learning he had advanced cancer with just a few months to live. The entire family decided to organize a special dinner where each family member shared how much we loved dad and expressed gratitude for what he meant to each of us. The difficult memories faded and were not relevant. In those moments, only love mattered.

I go on many calls as a first responder chaplain where death comes suddenly, with no opportunity for goodbyes or words of love to exchange. The greatest wisdom I must pass along from my years as a chaplain on the frontlines of life's greatest tragedies is do not leave love left undone. There may be things you do not accomplish, attain, or achieve in this world. But do not leave this world with the regret that you could have loved more.

Some years ago, I discovered Bronnie Ware, who is a nurse who spent many years working in palliative care, caring for patients in the last 12 weeks of their lives. She recorded their dying epiphanies in a blog, which later became a book called, *The Top Five Regrets of the Dying: A Life Transformed by the Dearly Departing*. She summarized these regrets into statements she most commonly heard from people close to death. One of the regrets were, "I wish I'd had the courage to express my feelings."

A common opinion about men is that we do not express our emotions well or at all. Guilty as charged! At least this has been true for most of my life. My father was not an emotionally expressive person. I sometimes tell people jokingly that I once thought I saw my father having a feeling, but it turned out I was wrong—his eyes got watery because of spring allergies. Even dad's anger was not so much an "expression" but an eruption. Having grown up with two brothers and involved in sports, I was also sufficiently conditioned into the mindset of sucking it up, showing no weakness or sentimentality, and enduring difficulties with steely resolve.

My relationship with my father was more behaviorally based than emotionally based. We did activities together—playing sports, fishing, running errands, chores, going someplace, but we did not do a lot of extraneous talking, especially not on a personal level that involved expressing feelings.

Even with all the research that shows how expressing emotions is central to building healthy, whole, and close relationships, I believe it is self-evident through the most basic personal reflection. We experience the world through our physical senses, thoughts and mental formations of our mind, and a more effective mode of various feeling tones. Emotions are the bare affective quality of an experience. Avoiding, denying, and repressing feelings means you are doing violence against life itself by insisting that you only engage the world through the activity of your body and machinations of the mind.

The most fulfilling, meaningful, profound, and transcendent experiences of life require the activation of our feelings, and emotional openness, availability, and vulnerability. The experience of beauty, art, and music, fully knowing another person, our capacity for self-knowledge that is critical for personal growth and wellbeing, and the ability to live compassionately and courageously, all require an emotive connectivity.

The church is known for asking the WWJD? question—What would Jesus DO? But have you ever wondered WWJF?—What would Jesus feel?

Did Jesus ever have that sinking feeling—that stone-cold thud in the bottom of your gut when someone you love is tragically ripped out of your life? Did he ever lay in bed at night, weary and overwhelmed with all the sorrow of the world, and wonder, "What's the point?" Did Jesus ever feel that crushing blow of being wounded by the one he trusted most? Did he ever feel like an outsider and silently suffer the deep ache of loneliness? Did Jesus grieve over those things he could not change, and was it ever so unbearable that he wept and wailed, and cried that cry that is so deep that no sound comes out at all? Did Jesus ever miss someone so terribly that he felt as if he had been torn in two? Did he ever hurt so badly that he thought he might die, and wanted to?

I believe Jesus did not spare himself from feeling all of that and more.

I learned a lot of theology about Jesus in seminary, which we referred to as "Christology" and involved themes such as hypostasis, dyophysitism, Trinitariansim, Christus Victor, the cosmic Christ, and many more. But in my view, the most profound and powerful verse in Scripture about Jesus is only two words, "Jesus wept."

Jesus did not theologize or spiritualize the human experience of life. He tasted the depths of it—the loveliness and ugliness, tragic and triumphant, joy and heartache. Jesus leaned into life and felt it deeply. He met others in their moments of elation and suffering, good fortune and loss, celebration and grief, abundance, and loss. There is something between living in denial and being swallowed whole by the pain and suffering of human existence, and Jesus lived there.

Why did Jesus do this? Because this is what it means to be human. You do not get to pick and choose. It is all of it.

It is okay to feel what human beings feel. We laugh, cry, dance, feel ecstasy, even feel despair. It is how we know the world. It is how we live inside of our hearts and not dissociated from them.

Being Jesus means that we go through life embracing it all fully and feeling it all deeply. That we do not hide and try to protect ourselves. That we live. That we show up. That we laugh. That we cry. That we hurt. That we heal. That we care. That we love. And we wake up the next morning and sign up for it all over again.

I learned many years ago that my most significant contribution when called to a dreadful scene as a first responder chaplain is to be there fully. Not just there in my head, not just there to "do" something to manage the situation, but to connect with another human being in what they are feeling in those moments. My way of serving those who are suffering heartache and grief is not by trying to somehow explain it with God or divert or deflect what they are feeling, but to be fully there and connected with them in it. This means I must be capable of accessing my own emotions, able to receive and hold the emotions of others, and willing to express what I feel in tangible and understood ways.

I sat at my father's bedside for several hours until I witnessed his last breath. I held his hand and spoke my feelings of love and gratitude for him. I wept at his passing with a heartache so deep that it left a cavity of sadness inside me that is still there. But I also feel a wholeness from the experience of having been fully there with dad for his final hours, minutes, heartbeats and breaths of his life. Not just there in my head, but there in my heart and feeling it all deeply.

King Solomon wrote in the Book of Ecclesiastes that there is a "time for everything", which includes both beauty and sorrow. But beauty and sorrow are not necessarily two completely different and separate things. Just when life delivers a blow that feels like it will be the end of you, you discover it actually helped unravel a little bit more of who you really are.

One moment a tidal wave of change turns your life upside down into something you hardly recognize, but then strangely provides a clearing for you to create the life you really wanted in the first place. Sometimes life is a path of self-destruction, sabotaging yourself at every turn and wrecking relationships as you go... that is, until you finally crack, break, and hit rock-bottom from where your journey of true healing begins.

Just when everything you were so certain of in life, and everything you placed your trust, faith and security in comes crashing to the ground... one day sifting through the rubble of what's left you find a couple of pieces to put together in a different way, add a few new pieces, and you're on your way to building something new, filled with possibilities.

And yes, there are those gut-wrenching moments when life strikes you down with a heartache so deep that feels you can never recover from, but then there's that song, breeze, sunset, hug, or something you catch out of the corner of your eye that mysteriously lets you know you're going to be okay... and you laugh even as the tears of heartache fall.

Do you see what I'm getting at here? There is a time for everything—that's the bad news... that's the good news.

Life!

Sometimes you mourn, sometimes you dance.

Sometimes it feels like it's all getting away from you, sometimes it comes together in ways you never imagined were possible.

Sometimes you give your heart, sometimes you withhold it.

Sometimes you search, sometimes you give up.

You hold one, you let go.

Sometimes you're the one delivering the blow, sometimes you're the one applying the balm.

Sometimes you break the silence, sometimes you step back and say nothing.

Do you see?

Stretch out a continuum between love and hate, between peace and war, and realize that you will not be spared. Life—you can run but you can't hide. Sometimes you're the one instigating it, sometimes it is callously and randomly thrust upon you without your choosing.

Faith is that something good is always there for you to find. In the living and dying, loving and hating, laughing and crying, dancing and mourning, tearing and mending, brokenness and building... it will be there. Sometimes you'll have to fight for it or be still enough to hear it or feel it but it will be there. Like a light breeze across your face, something will mysteriously whisper that you are loved, and tell you the story of how goodness and beauty prevail.

The metaphor of "father" to describe God makes sense to me now in a way it did not before. The term is meant to indicate God's personal connection to the world and all human beings. Lest we think of God as some detached, removed, impersonal, remote, and indifferent entity, force, or equation, Jesus addressed God as "Abba Father"—a term that describes an intimate, tender, and unbreakable parental bond.

There are three times in the New Testament when this reference to God is used. Jesus used it in the moment of his greatest darkness and suffering, during the circumstances that led to his brutal death. The Apostle Paul used the term "Abba Father" in his Epistle to the Romans, explaining that religion's way of conceiving God as a master and tyrant to obey and fear was false, and that God instead should be likened to a father who loves and seeks the wellbeing of his children. Paul also uses the term in his Epistle to the Galatians to bring focus to our identity in God's eyes as one unconditionally beloved of God. Brennan Manning wrote, "My identity as Abba's child is not an abstraction or a tap dance into religiosity. It is the core truth of my existence."

Rembrandt's final work of art depicted a parable in the Bible, depicting God as a father. *The Return of the Prodigal Son* is an oil painting that this Dutch master artist completed in two years before his death in 1669. Rembrandt was moved by the parable, and he made a variety of drawings, etchings, and paintings on the theme that spanned decades, beginning with a 1636 etching. The completed painting is now curated at the State Hermitage Museum in Saint Petersburg, Russia.

In the painting, the son has returned home in a wretched state from travels in which he has wasted his inheritance and fallen into poverty and despair. He kneels before his father in repentance, wishing for forgiveness and a renewed place in the family, having realized that even his father's servants had a better station in life than he. His father receives him with a tender gesture. His hands seem to suggest mothering and fathering at once; the left appears larger and more masculine, set on the son's shoulder, while the right is softer and more receptive in gesture.

Art historian H. W. Janson writes that Prodigal Son, "... may be Rembrandt's most moving painting. It is also his quietest—a moment stretching into eternity. So pervasive is the mood of tender silence that the viewer feels a kinship with this group. That bond is perhaps stronger and more intimate in this picture than in any earlier work of art."

Henri Nouwen, a Dutch priest and theologian, saw a poster of Rembrandt's painting *The Return of the Prodigal Son* that made such a deep impression on him that he decided to see the painting personally and traveled to Saint Petersburg (Leningrad at that time) to visit the Hermitage Museum where it is kept. This resulted in a several-day contemplation of the painting, which prompted him to author a book of the same name. *The Return of the Prodigal Son* was ranked as one of the 100 best Christian books of all time.

In the book Nouwen writes about Rembrandt's painting, "The true center of Rembrandt's painting is the hands of the father. On them all light is concentrated; on them the eyes of the bystanders are focused; in them mercy becomes flesh; upon them forgiveness, reconciliation, and healing come together, and, through them, not only the tired son, but also the worn-out father find their rest."

And so, it is that one of the most celebrated works of art in all of history is a rendering of God as father, full of deep feeling, intimacy, tenderness, and love.

I learned a lot about grief through the loss of my father, but I still miss my dad. There are days when I pull out old picture albums and look through fading photographs of us from baseball games and fishing trips. I am a father now, with sons and daughter of my own. Fatherhood is not for the faint of heart!

We have all heard the phrase "like father, like son." The phrase implies that a son's character or behavior can be expected to resemble that of his father. On more than one occasion Jesus insisted that any person could attain an accurate understanding of God by observing him and the life he lived.

The person Jesus was, and his life are a sharp contrast to the religious establishment of his day. Religion made people feel there was no chance of ever being good enough to earn God's love, but what they felt from Jesus is that they could never be bad enough to lose God's love. Religion has told people they were undeserving, unworthy, and perpetually falling short in God's eyes, but with Jesus they felt acceptance, kinship, belonging and solidarity. Religion laid a heavy burden on people with rituals to observe, rules to follow, laws to keep, and leaders to obey, but people learned from Jesus that they could simply live a life of love as he did, and that there was nothing more important than this. Religion held a view of the world that divided up life into "sacred" and "secular," and people into "us" and "them", but people walked away from Jesus with new eyes seeing God in everything and everyone, including themselves.

Jesus once said, "If you've seen me, you've seen the father."

Maybe "father" is not such a bad metaphor after all.

CHAPTER 19

ALWAYS AND NEVER

Brian Anderson was 26 years old when he was told he had terminal pancreatic cancer. He had kept this a secret from his family for six months. His mother and sister learned of his illness in the suicide note Brian left after he took his life, which they found after a six-hour drive to spend a week with him at his apartment in Southern California. With only a brief time left to live, Brian did not want to put himself or his family through the ordeal of his death by cancer.

It was after midnight and a light rain fell as several police and emergency vehicles with flashing lights were lined up in the parking lot outside the apartment building. Several other curious and concerned residents had come out to see what had happened. I stood with the mother and daughter outside in the freezing rain as investigators processed the scene inside. Mom was heartbroken that her son had not told her about his cancer, and that he had suffered this burden on his own, and then surrendered his life and left this world by himself and alone.

As you have read in this book, cases of suicide are a common occurrence in my work as a first responder chaplain. Suicide is a complicated issue, especially as it relates to the realm of God and religion, which is the framework I frequently find myself in. Quite often as a chaplain at a scene where a person has taken their life, I will be asked by their loved ones about my views of suicide based upon God and faith. One time a father of a teenage boy who killed himself was traumatized by a religious belief he was taught that suicide is an "unpardonable sin"—an act that will not be forgiven by God and punished by eternal hell.

Religion historically has had a dicey stance on suicide. Islam clearly forbids suicide. Jewish views on suicide are mixed. In Orthodox Judaism, suicide is forbidden by Jewish law, and viewed as a sin. In Hinduism, suicide is spiritually unacceptable, considered a violation of the code of ahimsa (non-violence) and therefore equally sinful as murdering another.

Christian doctrine has by and large held that suicide is morally wrong, despite the absence of clear Scriptural guidance regarding the matter. There has been much debate over the Christian view on suicide, with early Christians believing that suicide is sinful and an act of blasphemy. In more recent times, some Christian churches reject this idea, while others still espouse and teach this view.

In the fifth century, St. Augustine wrote the book *The City of God*, making with it Christianity's first overall condemnation of suicide. His biblical justification for this was the interpretation of the commandment, "Thou shalt not kill," which he included the killing of oneself. Suicide, Augustine determined, was an unrepentable sin. This conclusion was codified in the medieval doctrine that suicide nullified the person's relationship to God.

In the sixth century, suicide became a secular crime. In 1533, those who died by suicide were accused of a crime and denied a Christian burial. By 1562, all suicides were punished in this way. In 1693, even attempted suicide became an ecclesiastical crime, which could be punished by excommunication, with civil consequences following. In the 13th century, Thomas Aquinas denounced suicide as an act against God and as a sin for which one could not repent.

For the majority of the past two millennia, the Catholic Church has taught that suicide is a sin against God that has dire penalties.

Those who grew up Roman Catholic might have heard that suicide is a mortal sin that irretrievably sends people to hell. Those who had committed suicide were unable to be buried on sacred ground or receive a funeral Mass. Paragraphs 2280-83 of the Catechism of the Catholic Church deal with the question of why suicide is wrong: "We are stewards, not owners, of the life God has entrusted to us and, thus, our lives are not ours to dispose of." It is only relatively recently, with a heightened understanding of mental illness, stress, and emotional distress, that the Church's positioned has softened. Lest one judge the Catholic Church on this issue, Protestant Reformers, including Calvin, also condemned suicide.

In the 1990s, during the tenure of Pope John Paul II and for the first time, the Catechism of the Catholic Church acknowledged that, "Grave psychological disturbances, anguish, or grave fear of hardship, suffering, or torture can diminish the responsibility of the one committing suicide."

Does the Bible teach suicide is a sin? Many people assume the Bible condemns taking one's own life. However, even a careful reader will search in vain for any explicit prohibition of self-killing in the Bible. In fact, the biblical attitude toward suicide ranges from ambivalence to praise.

There are seven suicides in the Bible. Of the seven suicides reported in Scripture, most familiar are Saul, Samson, and Judas. Saul committed suicide to avoid dishonor and suffering at the hands of the Philistines. He is rewarded by the Israelites with a war hero's burial, there being no apparent disapproval of his suicide. And while there is no hero's burial for Judas Iscariot, Scripture is once more silent on the morality of this suicide of remorse. The suicide of Samson has posed a greater problem for Christian theologians. Both Saint Augustine and Saint Thomas Aquinas wrestled with the case and concluded that Samson's suicide was justified as an act of obedience to a direct command of God.

The first comprehensive modern defense of suicide was John Donne's Biathanatos in 1608. Not intended for publication, *Biathanatos* drew upon an array of classical and modern legal and theological sources to argue that Christian doctrine should not hold that suicide is necessarily sinful. He constructed an argument using the logic of Christian thought to suggest that suicide is not contrary to the laws of nature, of reason, or of God. Were it contrary to the law of nature mandating self-preservation, all acts of self-denial or privation would be similarly unlawful. Moreover, there may be circumstances in which reason might recommend suicide. Finally, Donne observes, not only does Biblical Scripture lack a clear condemnation of suicide, Christian doctrine has permitted other forms of killing such as martyrdom, capital punishment and killing in wartime.

As a former Christian pastor and now as a first responder chaplain, I have officiated countless funerals and memorial services, including many for those who have committed suicide. Understandably so, the question of the afterlife almost always comes up in these instances. Regardless of how uncertain or vague a person's views are of the afterlife, the issue comes into sharp focus at the death of a loved one. Suddenly, the idea of an eternal heaven or hell feels pressing and poignant.

The church's stance on heaven and hell has been just as complicated as its position on suicide. For example, the most common view of hell associated with the Christian church is that some humans will never be reconciled to God and will therefore remain separated from God forever, and that hell is a realm where they receive retribution in the form of everlasting torment. But there are also those who hold a view of universal reconciliation, which is the doctrine that all sinful and alienated human souls—because of divine love and mercy—will ultimately be reconciled to God.

The doctrine of universal reconciliation views Bible verses such as 1 Corinthians 15:22 as a basis for their position. Apostle Paul wrote, "For as in Adam all die, so also in Christ shall *all* be made alive." Notice the word "all." Christians who hold the universalist view point out that the word "all" comes up a lot. Colossians 1:19-20 reads, "For in Christ *all* the fullness of God was pleased to dwell, and through him to reconcile to himself *all* things, whether on earth or in heaven." Note again the "all." And in Romans 5:18, "Then as one man's trespass led to condemnation for *all* men, so one man's act of righteousness leads to acquittal and life for *all* men."

In the first 600 years of Christian history, researchers have identified six main theological schools concerning the ideas of how the world would be restored to its original or primordial condition of perfect harmony, peace, and flourishing. Four of them were Universalists, one taught "conditional immortality," and the last taught Eternal Hell. Many early church fathers have been quoted as embracing the ultimate reconciliation of God with all creation. Those that did not embrace the teaching, such as Augustine, acknowledged that it was a common enough belief among Christians of the day. Origen of Alexandria (184 – 253), was an early Christian scholar who advocated the belief that all creatures will finally be restored to God. Origen believed that the end would be a complete return to the beginning. The concept of a final restoration of all souls particularly had large appeal in the East during the fourth and fifth centuries.

The view of hell as God's eternal punishment turns on the Hebrew term "Sheol," which is translated as "Hades" in the Greek New Testament. Some Christian scholars point out that this term is erroneously taught as meaning eternal torment. They further assert that neither should the Greek word for hell in the New Testament (Gehenna) be understood this way, and that these references are intended to convey or represent the anguish and suffering that results when one alienates themselves from relationship with God.

It is beyond the scope of this book to lay out the various interpretations of the Bible with respect to the afterlife and the doctrine of hell, as well as the many different views of the church and Christians on this subject throughout Christian history.

Despite having studied theology academically, one day I realized that I still had not read my Bible closely enough. 1 John 4:8 states, "God is love." The middle word is the important one, "is" love. It is not that God DOES loving things; God IS love. There is never a moment when God is not love.

God's love is not tied to the performance-based system that religion is fond of teaching. God's love is not a reaction to your actions or beliefs. God's love is not a spigot that turns off and on based on the accuracy of your theology, how religious you are, or how far you have progressed on your journey. You do not determine God's love. You have absolutely no bearing upon it. God's love is not a response, reaction, or choice. God IS love. This is why God's love is unconditional—it is based on who he is, not what you do.

Unconditional love is the underlying, unchanging, and fundamental fact. God's love does not fluctuate. It cannot be earned or lost. It is never threatened. God's unconditional love is available to all people, all the time, everywhere. Of course, God is countless things—just, wise, powerful, beautiful, timeless, infinite, glorious—but the one aspect of God that seems to pull rank is love. Of all God's attributes, the greatest of these is love. Jesus told people if they wanted to understand who God really was to look closely at him. And what did they see? Love. What did they hear in his teaching? Love. What was the point of the stories and parables he told about God? Love.

The other afternoon I was rooting through our warzone attic searching for my saltwater spinning rod, when I found stacks of boxes with notebooks of old sermons in them. It is hard to say how many sermons and messages I gave as a pastor all those years, every Sunday morning, Sunday evening, and Wednesday night. Though some pastors recycle sermons, which is reusing a sermon they have given before. I was never able to give the same message twice. It just never felt right. It almost felt like cheating or taking the easy way out.

As a first responder chaplain I have officiated countless funerals and memorial services. In each one I basically give the same message. I have led funeral services for children who drowned in backyard pools, teenagers who took their own lives, fathers and mothers killed in car accidents, and senior adults who perished in fires and floods. But every time, I give the same message. It is not that I am not creative or thoughtful enough to come up with something different. It is because I discovered there was really only one message to ever give. And that was the message of love.

Over the years of my service as a chaplain on the front lines of life's most gruesome and heartrending tragedies, there have been times when I have questioned the point of it all and the place of God in it. Erich Fromm wrote, "Love is the only sane and satisfactory answer to the problem of human existence."

For many years I wanted to save the world from all this suffering. But then I learned that the world does not want to be saved, it wants to be loved. That is how you save it. Eventually a person comes to understand that love heals everything, and love is all there is. On our way out of this world we will look back and realize it was always about love. And if you take the Bible at its word, you would have to say it was always God because God is love.

The Bible says that love always perseveres.

Always.

It also says that love never fails.

Never.

CHAPTER 20

15 THINGS, THEN GOD

If I started removing things from your life, at what point would you stop me because you could not imagine wanting to live without them?

Take your possessions. You could let go of many belongings and still want to live. It wouldn't be too difficult to part with old clothes or books, clutter in your attic or garage, worn furniture, or cabinets filled with kitchenware you rarely use. It would be a little more painful to give up more significant possessions like your home or car, expensive jewelry, your favorite recreational toys like a boat or motorcycle, or your television, iPhone, or laptop, but I doubt you would conclude that life was not worth living without them.

Or let's take people. Who would you be able to live without? Of the eight billion human beings on earth, many of them could disappear and it would not impact your life. Acquaintances and strangers, we cross paths with daily are not necessarily integral to our lives. If your mail carrier retired, the familiar grocery cashier quit, or your neighbor moved, it would not be reason enough to give up on life. If you tragically lost someone you love, it would be devastating, and you might even for a time feel life was not worth living. But I have seen many cases where a person who suffered catastrophic loss worked through a grieving process and found renewed meaning, purpose, and passion in life.

What about your health? At what point would the loss of physical wellbeing cause you to question if life was worth living? We all experience a gradual decline of health in aging. Our eyesight and hearing may worsen, our mobility and activity level often declines, arthritis or osteoporosis may arise, various aches and pains pop up. But what if a stroke caused you a permanent disability or you were diagnosed with Parkinson's disease or discovered you had a terminal cancer? Would you feel that life would not be worth living?

What if you were in a state where the only thing you could do was lay in bed, and move your eyes up and down to respond "yes" or side to side, to indicate "no"? If everything else had been stripped away and this was the only thing you could do, would you feel that life would be worth living?

My answer to that question is: "No." That is, until I met Chris.

Approaching three decades of being a first responder chaplain, I have met about every tragic situation imaginable. I am personally impacted every time I step into the world of another human being who has suffered catastrophic loss or hardship. But rarely am I surprised or caught off guard by the specific circumstances I find because it is likely that I have encountered a similar situation previously.

But I was not prepared for Chris.

Fourteen years ago, Chris was diagnosed with Multiple Sclerosis. MS is a disease that damages the nerve cells in the brain and spinal cord. It is the most common immune-mediated disorder affecting the central nervous system. 1 million people in the US live with MS. There is no known cure for Multiple Sclerosis. MS develops in stages. Most people never experience the advanced stage and will likely remain mobile. But not Chris.

For Chris it started with muscle weakness, tremors, difficulty with coordination and balance, and problems with walking and standing. He began having vision problems that led to blindness, and difficulty speaking that resulted in aphasia, the inability to speak. His physical deterioration advanced to complete paralysis. He retained partial hearing and the full functioning of his mind, but every other muscle in his body ceased to work except the heart and lungs allowing him to breathe and circulate oxygen to his brain. Today, the only thing Chris can do with his body is move his eyes to indicate "yes" or "no". Only his eyes respond to the wishes of his mind, with one exception—his smile. Chris' mantra all through this awful ordeal over the years has been, "MS sucks, but God is good!" And boy can Chris still smile!

What if this was you? If you had been reduced to life in a bed with only the movement of your eyes, would you consider life worth living? Can you imagine anything close to happiness in that condition? How could any of us still put on a smile?

It was partly a chaplain call and partly a personal request when I was asked to take a two-hour shift to sit with Chris to relieve his wife, Katie, who had to pick up her kids from school, which was closing early due to bad weather. Chris was recently moved into a convalescent facility, which cares for people with end-stage MS. I met Chris and Katie years ago through our mutual involvement at a local church, and became aware of her husband's early battle with MS. We soon discovered that we lived in the same neighborhood and our kids were the same ages.

I can only imagine how the worsening of Chris's condition with three small children would have put a strain on Katie and the kids. Given the whole tragic ordeal, it would be understandable if Katie, not to mention Chris himself, would be struggling to make sense of all this considering God. A popular Christian worship song says, "God is good all the time." I wonder if this is what Chris is thinking as he lies in bed unable to do anything but move his eyes, never again being able to hold his wife or children in his arms or even speak to them. Or if Katie is singing this worship song in her car as she is hauling her children to school events and doctor's appointments as a single mom, trying to hold down a job with mounting financial pressures, while caring for a husband with permanent complete paralysis. God is good ALL the time?

I gently pushed open the cracked door to Chris's room, and was greeted by Katie. She was grateful that I would sit with Chris for a couple of hours. I asked how he was doing, and she filled me in on the latest developments. He had been having some difficulty breathing, but doctors were not overly concerned by it. A common cold could end Chris' life with respiratory failure.

It is interesting what people are prone to share with you, knowing you are an ordained minister and chaplain. All these years I could at any time understand if Katie were to feel betrayed and abandoned by God, and expressed her anger, disillusionment, and doubt in God in the face of their grim and demoralizing circumstances. But it never came.

Katie shared with me a couple of conversations she and Chris had before his MS had progressed to an advanced stage. They had no illusions about what the later stages of his disease would entail. Doctors warned them that Chris's condition could deteriorate to complete paralysis. Katie shared that she and Chris had determined that they would receive each day as a gift from God and would take each new development as an invitation to know God more deeply. Huh? Not the bitterness I expected. MS sucks, but God is good. Really?

Katie also shared with me a conversation she had with an acquaintance. Apparently, this person could not understand how Katie believed in God at all. They asked her what kind of God would allow MS, not to mention all illness, poverty, war, and suffering in the world. The person adamantly denied a belief in any God and questioned how Katie could. There are no shortage of people who think this way, and many times I have been questioned about how I can believe in God, given all the tragedy I see as a first responder chaplain. But rarely will someone like this be brazen enough to challenge a person directly with respect to their personal beliefs in God, like this individual did with Katie.

She shared that her first reaction was one of shock, coupled with a tinge of anger. Who has the audacity to question what another person finds meaningful? The idea has never stuck with Katie that God should be blamed for the hardships and suffering of the world or used as evidence that God does not exist. In Katie's mind, the world's problems are either an inevitable aspect of the human experience or caused by humans themselves. Katie shared with this person that spirituality and God were central components of her life, and a source of strength, joy, hope, compassion, and purpose, regardless of her circumstances. She shared that every time she looks over her life, there are countless ways God was real to her. Katie told this person that she was not afraid to admit this, or how her beliefs challenged her to live more humbly, with grace and gratitude.

I find it curious that many times people approach and debate the issue of God and suffering in theological, philosophical, and intellectual terms. It becomes a mental puzzle, trying to piece together the soundest argument either for or against God. Entire libraries could be filled solely with scholarly books that analyze and formulate various positions on questions of how to square the existence and character of God with evil and suffering in the world.

What is interesting about someone like Katie is that she takes as her primary reference point about God to be her direct and personal experience of God or how God has been real to Katie in her experience of life. One way says, I must first construct a coherent human intellectual understanding of God for permission to claim and live as if God exists. Katie's way is, because I have encountered God directly and God is real to me in my experience of life, my starting point is that God exists, and I am open to what that might mean in any given moment.

USED TO GO TO CHURCH

While theologians and philosophers debate God and suffering in the halls of academia, people like Katie are able to move beyond questioning God in times of suffering, they look for God.

Katie glanced down at her watch, and saw it was time to head off to get her kids from school. She told Chris I would be sitting with him for a while, and she would be back in a couple of hours. After kissing Chris on the forehead, she said to call if anything came up.

The moment Katie left the room and closed the door behind her, I felt nervous, anxious, and uncertain about the whole situation. How was I going to spend two hours with someone who could not move or talk but was fully conscious and aware? How do you communicate or interact with someone who can only move their eyes? Katie mentioned that Chris had a rough night and would likely sleep. I brought the newspaper to catch up on the latest current events and thought maybe I'd share those events with Chris if he were alert.

As I came to Chris' side he glanced up at me, his eyes were wide open, and he was alert as he could be showing off that big smile. He definitely did not seem too interested in sleeping. I wondered what Chris might be thinking as he laid there. Then I began contemplating all the reasonable "yes" or "no" questions I could ask him.

Chris had been a high school history teacher. As mentioned, we got to know him and Katie through our affiliation with an area church. Our kids and their kids were about the same age, and they became friends. One endearing characteristic of Chris's personality was his hilarious sense of humor. He could find amusement in about any situation of life. Sometimes Chris would poke fun at himself and his MS. I am not sure why, but he always wanted to share his latest MS humor with me. Once he said, "Nick, I'm going to start an MS CrossFit club." Another time he walked up beside me, and nonchalantly said, "So Nick, two MS guys walked into a bar; wait, wheeled into a bar." Chris once put his own twist on a Bible verse, "My body is a temple.

A Temple of doom." I never met anyone who could have such a sense of humor while suffering at the same time

I gently placed my hand on his arm and the only thing that came to mind to say with a slight grin on my face was, "Dude, you got some serious bed head!" A quivering smile filled his face and his breathing pattern intensified. Smiling and laughing was his forte. Chris's reaction broke the heaviness of the moment for me, which of course made me laugh and then him all the more. I was concerned that I needed to calm him down. Besides a common cold, his laughing bouts could do him in some day.

There we were in a convalescent facility having a moment together, cracking up hard! Not exactly what I had expected.

Then suddenly out of nowhere, a surge of sorrow rushed up from the bottom of my gut like a freight train and pushed through my chest and throat and into my eyes with a force that required every ounce of energy I had to contain. For the last ten years Chris has been unable to move, eat, or speak, but now he was smiling and laughing. How is that possible? How can a person in his situation and condition ever have reason to do either?

On the nightstand next to his bed, Chris had a picture of Katie and the kids. There was also a book, *Guns, Germs, and Steel: The Fates of Human Societies*. It figures he would be reading a history book. I asked him if he wanted me to read to him for a while, and he shifted his eyes "yes." I opened the book at the bookmark and started to read, "History, as well as life itself, is complicated; neither life nor history is an enterprise for those who seek simplicity and consistency." Is not that the truth! Life can be perplexing, unpredictable, and uncertain. Neither Chris nor so many others I have encountered as a first responder chaplain could have ever foreseen the circumstances of tragedy, hardship, and loss that befell them.

I continued reading the book aloud to Chris. Every few pages, I would glance up to check his demeanor. After finishing two chapters I stopped and asked if he wanted me to continue reading, and he gave me a "yes" with his eyes. After getting through half of the next chapter, I glanced up at him and he was fast asleep. Quietly closing the book and returning it to the nightstand, I sat there studying his face as I pondered all that he had been through. Over all these years of being a first responder chaplain, I think those two hours I sat with Chris were some of the most uncomfortable and liberating I can remember.

There are times when I have considered how I would prefer to die. Like some of you, it would be nice to go peacefully, painlessly, or quickly. Chris's process of dying has been a distressing, debilitating, and painstaking deterioration. We are all living to die or dying to live! Self-awareness is a supreme gift, a treasure as precious as life itself. This is what distinguishes us as human beings. But it comes with a costly price; the wound of mortality. Our existence is forever shadowed by the knowledge that we will grow, blossom, and, inevitably diminish and die. Most of us live in a functional denial or convenient forgetfulness when it comes to the certainty of our own death.

I had to force myself not to indulge my imagination about what it might mean to be inside Chris's body. The thought of not being able to see or speak or move any part of my body was disturbing and frightening. How does a person not devolve into madness?

Chris has been laying in a bed for ten years unable to move, eat, or speak. But for ten years—day after day, hour after hour—Chris has been able to do the one thing for which he is still capable, think. He has kept the full capacity of his mind. Chris is fully aware of himself, his condition, and the inevitability of his death. I am not sure if this self-awareness should be taken as a blessing or a curse.

I had often wondered what Chris thought about all the time, but it felt too uncomfortable to ask him. It seemed too personal a question.

Some part of me was strangely afraid of what his answer might be. It would be unbearable to hear him express ten years of lost hopes and dreams, or sorrows and regrets. There were times when I thought of Chris's situation as some sort of solitary confinement. A person can get trapped in their own mind.

Chris's nurse quietly slid into the room to check if all was well. She joked about how accomplished Chris was as a professional nap taker. She said, "All that thinking can wear a guy out!" I guess it was a Freudian slip when I casually asked, "Wonder what he thinks about all the time?" She turned toward me and said, "I asked him one day. I went through a list of fifteen different things until I got to God, and he eyed me a yes. When he is not napping, that boy is thinking about God." With that, she said, "Let me know if you need anything" and slipped out of the room.

How much could I remove from your life before you would conclude that life was no longer worth living? What if you could no longer move, see, eat, or speak? Would life be worth living then? What I learned from my two hours with Chris is that what truly makes life meaningful cannot ever be taken away from you.

Viktor Frankl is a Holocaust survivor who endured four Nazi death camps including Auschwitz from 1942–45. In his book, *Man's Search for Meaning*, Frankl wrote, "Everything can be taken from a man but one thing: the last of the human freedoms—to choose one's attitude in any given set of circumstances, to choose one's own way."

A common Christian saying that misconstrues a verse from the Bible is, "God will never give you more than you can handle." Like most bumper-sticker theology, this saying is problematic in many ways. First, it implies that God is the one determining the severity of the difficulties and hardships you experience in life. According to the saying, God gives you these difficulties but only with a severity that God knows you are capable of withstanding. Secondly, it puts the full weight of enduring hardship on your shoulders, "God will never give you more than YOU can handle." In other words, it is your job to handle it.

The erroneous phrase is an unfortunate rendering of 1 Corinthians 10:13, which reads, "No testing has overtaken you that is not common to everyone. God is faithful, and he will not let you be tested beyond your strength, but with the testing he will also provide the way out so that you may be able to endure it." According to the verse, we are not alone in the difficulties and hardships we encounter in life. It is not like God is singling you out; life's hardships are common to everyone. It is the nature of our reality in the world that there will be times when life is tragic, grievous, and heartbreaking.

The verse points out that we are never left defenseless or abandoned in our times of greatest struggle and need because God has made a provision, which enables us to endure hardships but not be destroyed by them. In other words, knowing what the human journey would entail God equipped us with an ability that offers a way through every possible eventuality of the human experience.

It is what Viktor Frankl utilized in Nazi death camps, and what Chris depended upon in his bed, unable to move, see, or speak. What is it? The capacity and power of choice without constraint. Frankl wrote, "Between stimulus and response there is a space. In that space is our power to choose our response. In our response lies our growth and our freedom."

All your possessions could be destroyed in a fire. You could lose your loved ones in a tragic accident. Illness could devastate your health. You could lose your ability to move, see, or speak. But no circumstance can strip you of the choice to find meaning in life, honor your highest truth, fill your mind with what is noble and beautiful, and be an expression of love. No one could take away this choice from

Viktor Frankl. No one can take away this choice from Chris. Or me. Or you.

There are countless limitations we all experience in life. Many variables that affect our lives are outside our control. There are all sorts of factors that govern what we can or cannot do—our genetics, circumstances, abilities, available opportunities, and so on. Knowing this, God knit into the fabric of our being an ability that trumps everything else, the freedom to choose meaning, joy, love, beauty, peace, and compassion in any situation or circumstances. There is a creative capacity within each of us that works with the raw materials of life experience to create meaning, actualize our highest potentialities as image-bearers of God, and press out the transcendent dimensions of every moment and experience of life. We have the power to make beauty from ashes. Clive Barker wrote, "Any fool can be happy. It takes a human with real heart to make beauty out of the stuff that makes us weep." This is the heart and capability God has given us.

When Katie came back, Chris was still asleep. We chatted for a few minutes, and then I had to head off to a meeting across town at the police precinct. As I drove, the nurse's words were still hanging in my mind. She said, "I went through a list of fifteen different things until I got to God, and he eyed me a yes. That boy is thinking about God."

We all have a list of 15 things that make life a challenge, throw us off course, test our sanity, cause us anxiety, and sometimes knock us to our knees. But at the bottom of the list you will always find God. And as long as your mind is functioning, you can choose what really matters most in life. You can lose everything—every possession, every person, every security; you can even lose your ability to move, see, and speak, but you'll never lose your freedom of choice. This is God's gift to every human being. Life is not what happens to you. Our experience of life is ultimately determined by how we participate in life through choice.

GOD SHATTERS HIMSELF

My work as a first responder chaplain thrusts me into grim scenes of tragic heartbreak and suffering. In many cases where there has been loss of life, I am requested to lead a funeral or memorial service, which are also occasions of grief and sorrow. But as a chaplain, I am also asked at times to officiate more celebratory occasions such as births, anniversaries, and weddings.

I officiated the wedding ceremony of Kaesy and Justin. I met these two at a fundraising dinner for a group home in our community that uses a residential model to work with homeless youth. Licensed by the Department of Social Services, Justin managed this group home. As I became more involved and got to know both of them, one day they approached me to ask if I would lead their wedding ceremony. Yes!

Through the premarital counseling sessions I did with Kaesy and Justin, I grew to know them more deeply, believed in them as a couple, and loved them both. Over the years as a pastor and chaplain, I have officiated not a few wedding ceremonies in which I admittedly had my doubts about the wedding couple, and their relationship. Not so with Kaesy and Justin.

Kaesy and Justin were two very capable individuals—intelligent, creative, competent, and responsible. Most importantly, they were especially good at loving each other.

Kaesy was Justin's #1 fan, and Justin was convinced that Kaesy hung the moon. They built each other up and saw the best in each other. I noticed the way they genuinely valued one another's feelings and needs and worked together as a team. There was a true depth and intimacy to their bond. There was also a compelling passion to their relationship. Kaesy and Justin would never be accused of taking life or their relationship as a casual matter. They were all in! They leaned into life with gusto, embraced it all and each other fully, and never looked back. There was no love left undone with Kaesy and Justin.

I also saw conviction in Kaesy and Justin's relationship. This was not just some fun-loving, daydreamy, naive, impulsive, flimsy kind of deal. There was something rock-solid here. They had a dogged devotion to one another's well-being, and the dreams they shared together. I saw them weathering difficulties, challenges and adversity together. This was not a Kardiashian relationship, it was more like John and Abigail Adams. It was a bond and partnership of loyalty and conviction.

It did my heart good to witness the love story that Kaesy and Justin were creating and living together. Officiating their wedding was a beautiful, moving, and spiritual occasion that I will never forget. In my remarks at the wedding, I reminded those in attendance that despite all the things that are wrong in our world today, love is not one of them. Love is the one thing that is always right.

The greatest single need and desire of humankind is love. To love is the greatest power and freedom we possess. Every thought, word, and action motivated by love, changes the world. Love is the highest expression of what it means to be human. The chief characteristic of true spirituality is love. Virtually every religion and philosophy affirm the preeminence of love. Love is never the problem, it is always the solution. Love is never wrong; it is always right.

Despite Hollywood romances that come and go, true love is not merely some sappy, sentimental, starry-eyed, ivory-tower parallel universe. Love is tenacious. It has grit and staying power. Love is resolute. It has traction. Love protects and perseveres. Love does not cut and run, turn a blind eye, or remain silent. Love goes to the mat. Love is courageous. Love is not a spectator sport. Love is invincible. It cannot be defeated. You cannot kill it.

Martin Luther King, Jr. wrote, "I have decided to stick with love, for I know that love is ultimately the only answer to humankind's problems. And I am going to talk about it everywhere I go. I know it is not popular to talk about it in some circles today. And I am not talking about emotional bosh when I talk about love; I am talking about a strong, demanding love. For I have seen too much hate, and I say to myself that hate is too great a burden to bear. I have decided to love. If you are seeking the highest good, I think you can find it through love. And the beautiful thing is that we aren't moving wrong when we do it, because John was right, God is love. He who hates does not know God, but he who loves has the key that unlocks the door to the meaning of ultimate reality."

The wedding ceremony was magnificent, the reception was a hoot, and we sent Kaesy and Justin off for a life of love together!

On their one-year anniversary, Kaesy was diagnosed with cervical cancer.

Cervical cancer is considered the fourth most common cause of cancer and the most common cause of death for women. An estimated 13,800 women in the United States will be diagnosed with invasive cervical cancer this year. About 4,290 of those women will die. Cervical cancers can spread, most often to the regional lymph nodes, lungs, liver, bladder, and the vagina.

Kaesy battled hard. Justin never left her side. Once while Kaesy was in intensive care for abdominal bleeding, I parked my camper trailer at the hospital so Justin could get some much-needed sleep without being far away. We prayed fervently, but treatment after treatment failed. Kaesy suffered through surgery, chemotherapy, radiotherapy, and drug treatments, but doctors could not remove the cancer and it continued to spread. We prayed more, hoping for a miracle. But the miracle never came. She went into hospice care. A year later, Kaesy died.

When Kaesy was in her final days I was traveling abroad in India as part of a project that worked with AIDS victims and orphans. I received news that she was failing, and at once returned to the US. I made it home on the day she died but got to be with her one last time. I held Kaesy's hand, and told her how loved and special she was. She told me how grateful she was for her extraordinary life and was ready to surrender it to this world and move on to the next. Kaesy's final request was that I officiate her funeral service. I recalled that day she asked if I would officiate their wedding ceremony. Two years later I led Kaesy's funeral service.

It is a rare gift to understand that your life is wondrous, and that it will not last forever. I dedicate this book to Kaesy because she helped me learn this. All these years as a first responder chaplain I thought the deal was me helping others in their darkest hour of need. I certainly hope my presence and involvement in these tragedies made a difference. But I see now that these experiences have been instrumental in my own personal growth and life's journey.

I learned that faith is not always confidence that it will all work out, but it is deciding to live another day when it does not. Divine intervention is not necessarily a miracle handed down from heaven, but a simple act of caring offered by a human hand. I came to understand that feelings of grief, sorrow, and heartache are not meant to be anesthetized with elaborate theological constructions but given space to be fully felt and faced.

There was a time when I was angry with God about all the suffering he allowed in the world, until I realized that we are the ones who allow it, and conveniently blame God. I used to think that what made Jesus superior to the rest of us was his divinity but discovered instead that it is his humanity we fall short of. For me, church is no longer somewhere you go, but a way of being in the world.

God never promised that life would be without suffering. Rather, he promised that it would. We tend to think that the trick to happiness is to avoid suffering but Jesus said, "Blessed are they that mourn." We were not left defenseless against the sorrows of the world, but we were given the power to make beauty from ashes.

C.S. Lewis wrote, "My idea of God is not a divine idea. It has to be shattered time after time. God shatters it Himself." People are often told of the importance of knowing God, but I realize now that my mistake was assuming that I did. I once thought God was supposed to be a fixed and unchanging entity that I could count on for certain things in life. Now I realize that God is an open field of potential and possibility that spontaneously arises and offers itself in every moment.

Faith is not something made in Bible study classes at Church. It is formed on the frontlines of life's tragedies and forged in the crucible of suffering. Life holds its miracles, good arising from darkness chief among them. It was easy to think of myself as a hero for efforts as a first responder chaplain, until I realized there is no greater heroism than to keep living your life when circumstances do not readily offer any reasons for wanting to.

Two hours after Kaesy's funeral service, I received a call from dispatch about a tragic situation that involved loss of life, at which I was urgently needed. Helen Keller wrote, "Although the world is full of suffering, it is full also of the overcoming of it." What I learned is that God is equally present in the fullness of the suffering and the overcoming.

HEROES

I was putting the finishing touches on this book when the World Health Organization declared COVID-19 a pandemic. The next thing I knew, schools and colleges were shut down, professional sports seasons were cancelled, non-essential businesses closed their doors, Americans were told to stay at home, unfamiliar terms like "social distancing" and "shelter in place" became everyday language... and people started dying. As of this writing, there have been over 60,000 U.S. deaths from the coronavirus.

This microscopic infectious agent originating on the other side of the world has crippled our economy with mass unemployment and financial hardship. Our healthcare system, hospitals, first responders and medical professionals have been pushed to the brink. There are new warnings to expect a second wave of COVID-19 still to come. One thing is sure: life in America will never be the same again.

What has been the church's response?

Franklin Graham went on national television to declare that God was punishing humankind with the coronavirus because we have sinned against God and betrayed him. Graham said, "This pandemic is the result of a fallen world that has turned its back on God. People are dying from coronavirus because of the sin that is in the world." Meanwhile, American millionaire televangelist, Kenneth Copeland, claimed he could command the Satan-conceived coronavirus to vanish, and produced a made-for-tv "blowing away" service in which he "inhaled the mighty breath of God" and allegedly blew COVID-19 into oblivion.

The popular pastor John Piper argued that the pandemic is God's judgment on sinful cities and arrogant nations. Piper said, "God sometimes uses disease to bring particular judgments upon those who reject him and give themselves over to sin." A prominent church in Texas recently paid for a billboard to ask commuters: "Is the coronavirus a judgment from God?"

Another prominent clergyman, Ralph Drollinger, the Christian minister who leads a Bible study for members of President Donald Trump's Cabinet, wrote in a series of blog posts that a disease such as COVID-19 is "God's consequential wrath on our nation." Robert Jeffress, another high-profile Christian minister close to Trump, echoed this idea by warning, "All natural disasters can ultimately be traced back to sin."

I'm not saying that all churches and religious leaders responded as accusatory and irresponsibly as this, but these are the stories that trend in social media and grab the headlines in our nation's largest news organizations.

Many religiously unaffiliated people are too frustrated with the way Christians behave to give their churches a try. The Barna Group, one of America's leading polling organizations focused on religion, conducted a sweeping survey of the non-religious aged 16 to 29, and found that a new generation has grown skeptical of and frustrated with the Christian faith because of negative personal experiences with Christians whose words and actions seemingly misrepresent Christ. The notoriously poor behavior of Christians who consistently indict the world as spiritual law breakers has created a situation in which young people are saturating churches with their absence— worn out members don't want to stay, and spiritual seeking nonmembers don't want to start.

The title of this book, *Used to Go to Church*, came from my countless experiences at tragic and fatal scenes when I introduced myself as a first responder chaplain. Equating the term "chaplain" with God and religion, many times the person responded by saying that they "used to go to church." Given current societal trends, another accurate phrase would be "won't go to church." Fed up with Christians and churches, particularly in times of crisis, tragedy and suffering, an increasing number of people simply "won't go to church." Not now. Not ever.

The impact of the COVID-19 pandemic gave occasion to another phrase: not "USED TO go to church", not "WON'T go to church", but "CAN'T go to church." In the wake of the "shelter in place", "stay at home" and "social distancing" mandates, as coronavirus infections and deaths started climbing, churches were expected to cooperate by postponing public gatherings. Some churches refused to cancel worship services and move them online because, as one pastor put it, "Church is an essential business to God."

Post-coronavirus life in America will most assuredly be different. The coronavirus pandemic is causing fundamental changes to significant parts of our daily lives that will result in a new normal once COVID-19 is defeated. There have been only a handful of scenarios in recent American memory that have caused such sweeping changes to our culture, economy, and government. For many Americans, the COVID-19 crisis is equal in weight to 9/11 or the 2008 economic recession—two historic events of the 21st Century that brought forth new policy initiatives and reshaped the way we travel, think, and protect ourselves as a nation.

As we continue to combat this national emergency by shuttering nonessential businesses, closing schools, and encouraging Americans to stay home, we have found ourselves bracing for lasting changes to our society. American life as we know it has already been widely disrupted. No longer are most people congregating in bars or parks, dining out, or going into the office for work. It is hard to say what all this means for the future.

But I have also noticed something inspiring, redeeming, and beautiful that has arisen from this crisis. The cult of celebrity is vanishing. People are much more interested in celebrating the new heroes of our time: the healthcare workers on the frontline of the pandemic; the truckers and delivery drivers transporting essential items to Americans; the supermarket and pharmacy workers keeping stores open so we can get our essential supplies; factory, farm and warehouse workers keeping the wheels of industry turning; utility and tech workers; and, of course, our first responders and emergency services personnel.

The world will never be the same again. But the main thing that has changed during this difficult time is that people have reassessed what matters in their lives and discovered a new respect for the ordinary women and men who go to work every day to put their lives on the line for us and don't have the luxury of working from home or first-world problems such as sitting on the sofa for hours contemplating what to watch on Netflix.

For over twenty years as a first responder chaplain, I have worked alongside these kinds of heroes. Firefighters who selflessly run into burning buildings to save lives, and paramedics who unflinchingly rush into dangerous, chaotic and grisly scenes to perform life-saving measures. I have worked with police officers who are called upon to respond in emergencies, disasters, search and rescue situations, homicides, suicides, violence, criminal incidents, and threats to public safety. We can't forget our dispatchers who spend a career hearing nightmarish screams for help from callers who just witnessed a loved one dying. Throughout my career as a first responder chaplain

I have encountered countless ER doctors and nurses who tirelessly pour themselves into giving emergency medical care in grim and life-threatening scenarios.

It's not only that I have worked alongside these heroes in tragic and harrowing situations, but I have also had the opportunity to know them more personally in terms of their character and heart, what makes them tick, and who they are as wives and husbands, mothers and fathers, citizens and neighbors. I consider myself fortunate to be serving side-by-side with these brave men and women each time I am dispatched to an emergency scene of trauma and suffering.

The most sacred work I do as a first responder chaplain is to assist our heroes in dealing with the variety of emotions that come along with the job. My role is to help give them the tools to deal with such issues as PTSD, anxiety, depression, addictions, and relationship challenges. The COVID-19 pandemic has put a spotlight on the chronic stress and trauma that our medical professionals and first responders are subjected to each day.

The reality for first responders includes:

- They are exposed to highly stressful situations in the course of their routine duties.

- They have no control over the volume of calls they receive.

- They are often put in situations where they face overwhelming demands.

- They risk being seriously injured or killed in the line of duty.

- They will likely witness a peer being injured or killed in the line of duty.

- They witness horrifying events: crashes, severe injuries, and multiple death scenes—often involving infant deaths and entire families.

Suicide among first responders is on the rise. They are here for us, but who is there for them? My role as a first responder chaplain includes being someone who cares and listens with confidentiality, gives direct guidance, offers spiritual support, suicide prevention, marriage mediation, building resiliency, and anything else required to support our heroes in their time of need.

Maybe you are a first responder reading this right now. I want to thank you from the bottom of my heart for who you are and what you do.

Not many people think of church leaders, pastors and preachers as heroes. Instead, thinking of the examples I gave above related to prominent Christian leaders and COVID-19, we see them more as vanguards of the sin management problem they proclaim rather than the solution which would be far better served with mercy and grace. Rather than insisting upon holding church services in defiance of "stay at home" mandates, what would it look like instead if churches became actively engaged in supporting, aiding, and assisting those on the front-lines who are risking their own lives to save ours? While the government attempts to provide financial relief to some people through direct deposits and mailed checks, I wonder how many mega churches could marshal their financial resources to care for those in crisis, mobilize teams to help expedite critical and essential services, or support other critical COVID-19 efforts.

Why can't the church be a band of heroes? Shouldn't people of faith be "first responders" in their own right—risking their comfort to courageously be one of the first people to show up in the lives of hurting people to offer love, compassion, solidarity, and tangible assistance? We are all chaplains to each other, if we choose to be, when tragedy strikes in the lives of others we know and love. But also to the strangers and foreigners.

The Christian faith claims Jesus as its founder, and Jesus was this kind of hero. The love of Jesus was not some sappy sentimentality. The love that Jesus lived was tough as nails. There was grit in Jesus' love. It had traction and staying power. Jesus did not turn a blind eye, expect someone else to fix it, walk away, or cross over on the other side of the street. Love is not a spectator sport. Love says, "Nope, not on my watch, not here." Love shows up selflessly, courageously, and unflinchingly. Christians are fond of thinking of Jesus as a divine God but have seemed to miss the spirit of his life as a heroic human.

The notion of heroism is far more immediate and relevant to our daily lives than we might imagine. You do not have to become a front-page activist, launch a social revolution, be messianic, quit your job or join the Justice League to carry out a heroic action. Heroism is acting on behalf of a person in need or a cause you believe in, without personal gain and with awareness of likely sacrifices and costs. It might be a spontaneous and impulsive deed or may be a reflective and planned course of action. A person of any age can act heroically. You can cultivate the habit of standing up, speaking out and taking decisive action in challenging situations in your life.

The COVID-19 pandemic has shown us that the heroes who most inspire us do not wear capes, leap buildings, or have special powers. They are ordinary human beings who do extraordinary things. They take personal risks to help someone in need, stand up for their values, undertake a humanitarian effort or intervene in a time of tragedy or crisis. I'm thinking of firefighter and friend Chris who left his family and was released from our department to go volunteer in a New York City hospital as a peer support member to come alongside nurses and doctors who are suffering through a daily routine of losing patients to the coronavirus. That's what Jesus would do.

We have a duty to ourselves to perceive and live our heroic calling and be mindful of the consequences of our inaction. We are made to be heroes and denying this part of us has far-reaching implications. There is a hero in all of us. Taking heroic action gives expression to this deep-seated innate need we all have. When we are acting heroically, we realize the pinnacle of what it means to be human; this explains why heroic action is challenging, tests you, requires sacrifice, and costs you something. It is why heroic action transforms you and the world and is the crowning glory of a life lived well.

Used to go… won't go… can't go—when was it that we somehow thought of "church" as a place you go? COVID-19 got many Christians upset and incensed about being unable "to go to church", when we could have raised the bar on what it means to "be the church" in the world. "Church" is not on Sunday morning with a select few in attendance, church is everywhere, all the time, with everybody.

All of us are called to be first responders in our own way. A first responder is a person with specialized training who is among the first to arrive and aid at the scene of an emergency. You may not be specifically trained to rescue people from a fire, provide emergency and life-saving medical intervention, or abate a public threat, danger or crisis. But if you are a person of faith you believe yourself to be an expression or embodiment of the nature of God. That is what it means to be a manifestation of "God's image". God is the ground of our being. This means we are completely equipped to enter a world of need, suffering, hardship, tragedy and crisis, and be love, be hope, be compassion, be wisdom, be grace, be courageous, be generous, be useful… be heroes.

May it be so.

Many voices. One message.

Ingram Content Group UK Ltd.
Milton Keynes UK
UKHW021825270423
420897UK00010B/546